Economic Interactions of Pastoral Lowland and Highland Systems and Implications for Sustainable Livelihoods: A Case Study in Northeastern Ethiopia

FSS Research Report No. 7

Workneh Negatu

Forum for Social studies
Addis Ababa

ISBN: 978-99944-50-43-5

Forum for Social Studies (FSS)
P.O. Box 25864 code 1000
Addis Ababa, Ethiopia
Email: fss@ethionet.et
Web: www.fssethiopia.org.et

This Research Report was Published with the Financial Support of the Department for International Development (DFID, UK), the Embassy of Ireland, the Embassy of Denmark, and the Royal Embassy of Norway.

Table of Contents

List of Tables and Figures

Acknowledgements

My first acknowledgement and appreciation go to the Forum for Social Studies (FSS) that sponsored this research and helped me to achieve my long-standing ambition to investigate lowland-highland economic interactions and the implications for sustainable and secure livelihoods. I wish also to thank different individuals without whose support and cooperation my work would not have been completed. In particular, I wish to extend my thanks and appreciation to Mesfin Tadesse, who helped me a lot as a research assistant in hot and malaria-prone study areas. I also would like to thank Abnet Kebede, who helped me in gathering and compiling various documents, and the enumerators who spent days in interviewing pastoralists in the household survey. The Administration Offices and Offices for Conflict Prevention and Resolution, Agricultural and Rural Development Offices in Kewot and Ankober *woredas*, Pastoral and Rural Development Offices in Semurobi-Gelealo and Dulecha *woredas*. Administration Officers and agricultural experts in Argoba Liyu *woreda* all deserve my thanks for their help in providing valuable information and data.

Moreover, I acknowledge the key role played and guidance provided by the Chairperson of the Joint Peace Committee for the three *woredas* - Ankober, Argoba and Dulecha while moving from village to village and by linking me with relevant persons and officers. There are many pastoralists, farmers and experts whose names cannot be listed here for lack of space to whom I wish to convey my thanks and appreciation. Finally, my deep appreciation and acknowledgement go to the two anonymous reviewers of the first draft for their in-depth and thorough comments, which have helped me a lot to improve the research report. I am, however responsible for any errors and shortcomings in this report.

List of Acronyms and Abbreviations

CSA	Central Statistical Authority
DFID	Department of Foreign and International Development
FGD	Focus Group Discussion
FGM	Female Genital Mutilation
E.C.	Ethiopian calendar
IDS	Institute of Development Studies
KII	Key Informant Interview
MoARD	Ministry of Agriculture and Rural Development
MoFED	Ministry of Finance and Economic Development
NSA	Non-State Actors
PADET	Pastoral Association for Development in Ethiopia
PADD	Pastoralist Area Development Department
PCDP	Pastoral Community Development Program
PFE	Pastoralist Forum Ethiopia
SNNP	Southern Nations, Nationalities and Peoples (regional state)
SRG	Semurobi-Gelealo (one of the study *woredas*)
UN OCHA	United Nations Office for Coordination of Humanitarian Affairs- Pastoralist Communication Initiative
USAID	United States Agency for International Development

Glossary

Belg	Short and minor rainfall season (February to April)
Birr	Ethiopian currency
Gillie	Sword-like traditional weapon
Girgire	Young goat
Kebele	Lowest legal administrative unit
Meher	Long and main rainfall season (June to September)
Teff	Grass-like cereal crop
Timad	Farm land with size equivalent to a quarter of a hectare
Woreda	Administrative unit with authority higher than a *Kebele*; it comprises a set of *Kebeles*
Zuti	Name of the livestock marketplace in Shewarobit town
Masho	Local name for the tiny seeded pulse crop (mungbean)

1   Introduction

In Ethiopia, pastoralists reside in semi-arid and arid lowlands. The long-established multifaceted isolation compounded with negative effects of climate change, population growth and environmental degradation has severely undermined pastoral economic systems, livelihoods and food security. The poor integration of lowland and highland economic systems into the national economy has potentially hindered economic growth and livelihood diversification in pastoral systems.

On the basis of the existing conventional classification, about 61% of Ethiopia's land is lowland (below 1,500 meters above sea level), while 39% of it is highland (1,500 meters and more above sea level). The highland is inhabited by 85% of the human and 75% of the livestock population of the country. The lowland is climatically arid, semi-arid and sub-humid, while the highland is predominantly sub-humid and humid. The lowlands are generally characterized by relatively high temperature, drought, scarce rainfall and fragile arid and semi-arid ecology. The lowland-highland interface is a critical component of the lowland and highland production systems comprising elevations ranging from about 1,300 meters to 2,000 meters above sea level (Workneh, 2010). The interface domain ranges climatically from semi-arid lowland to sub-humid highland, and serve as platforms for economic and social interactions of lowlanders and highlanders.

The highland farming system in Ethiopia is oriented mainly towards the production of cereals and pulses, while the lowland system is engaged primarily in livestock production. Livestock production in the lowlands occurs in mobile pastoral and semi-mobile agro-pastoral systems in which both livestock and crop components are important. The distribution of livestock across lowland and highland systems in 2008 is shown in Table 1 below. As shown in the table, pastoralists own about 11 million heads of cattle, 6.5 million sheep, 15.2 million heads of goats and 2.3 million heads of camels in 2008.

Table 1: Livestock distribution in the highland and lowland areas of Ethiopia

| Type | Total livestock heads (in millions) | | | | Total |
| | Highland | | Lowland | | |
	In No.	%	In No.	%	In No.
Cattle	29.93	(73%)	11.07	(27 %)	41
Sheep	18.5	(74%)	6.5	(26%)	25
Goats	7.82	(34%)	15.18	(66%)	23
Chickens	NA	-	NA	-	41
Equines	NA	-	NA	-	5.7
Camels	0	-	2.3	(100%)	2.3

SOURCE: SOS Sahel, 2008

According to the 2007 population census (CSA, 2008), the population in pastoral dominated regions of Ethiopia is about 10.3 million. Of this the Somali and the Afar regions respectively have 4.44 million (43%) and 1.38 million (13.5 %) – pastoral population. The remaining pastoral population resides in Oromia, SNNP, Gambella, Benshangul-Gumuz region and Dire Dawa City Administration. With nearly 3.94 million inhabitants, the pastoral population residing in Oromia region is the second largest pastoral population in the country comprising 38% of the total pastoral population. In all cases, pastoral population includes urban population within the regions or zones referred.

Little et al. (2010) calculated the cash values of the home consumed livestock products on the basis of data on household income from 2000-2002 for five sites in southern Ethiopia. The result indicates that the cash value of home produced and consumed milk accounts for about 49% of household income, while the direct cash receipt from livestock sales stands for 16%. Overall, livestock and livestock products account for 37-87% of the total household cash income in different parts of the country (SOS Sahel, 2008).

At national level, export of livestock and livestock products is among the major earners of foreign exchange (SOS Sahel, 2008; PFE, 2004). The sub-sector's export commodities include live animals, meat and meat products, dairy products, hides and skins, leather products, honey and wax and civet (PFE, 2004). In Ethiopia, pastoralist and agro-pastoralist areas such as Borena, Afar and Somali regions, are considered to be the traditional source of livestock supplying 95% of livestock destined for export market (Belachew and Jemberu, 2003 cited in Getachew et al., 2008). At the same time, the sector is subjected to illegal cross-border livestock trade and large number of livestock is annually taken to Somalia, Djibouti and Kenya across the Ethiopian borders (SOS Sahel, 2008). This, of course, would have undesired effect of denying national earnings for Ethiopia and implies the need for designing strategies to capture the national earnings simultaneously benefiting the herders to gain economically in a legal trading framework.

Pastoral system also has immense environmental and ecological significances. The dry land ecology consists of different flora and fauna resources. For instance, the supply of breeding animal stock from the pastoral areas is an important input to the highland agricultural system. In Ethiopia, the Borena cattle breed has contributed significantly to national breeding programs and improvement of cattle productivity. Moreover, the lowlands and rift valley areas of Ethiopia, which are predominantly inhabited by pastoralists, are the habitat for many wildlife and endemic bird species that are a potential attraction for the tourism industry (SOS Sahel, 2008).

Pastoral communities are quite appreciated for their indigenous institutions and natural resource management practices. The institutions are used in resource use planning; enforcing rules on the use of shared resources and land; mobility and settlement patterns; disaster and risk mitigation and conflict management. They are, therefore, valued for their contribution to the very survival of the pastoral system, adaptation and resilience under difficult ecological conditions (SOS Sahel, 2008; Ayalew, 2001; Getachew, 2000).

In spite of the variations between lowland and highland systems in ecology, resource endowments and economic conditions, the communities in both lowland and highland economic systems commonly suffer from poverty, poor economic growth and low productivity. The pastoral system is particularly exposed to vulnerable livelihoods and food insecurity. Besides, the pastoral system is poorly integrated with the highland economic system. Due to infrastructural problems, subsistence oriented production system and cultural factors, the lowland and highland economic domains do not have adequate market and economic interactions. However, given that each economic system has its own comparative advantages in natural, socio-economic and cultural endowments, enhancing market and economic ties between lowland and highland systems would benefit both systems.

It is also envisaged that interactions between lowland and highland economic systems would contribute to prevention, mitigation and resolution of conflicts that may arise among different socio-cultural groups, particularly between lowland pastoralists and highland farmers. The causes of conflicts are connected with competition for resources, including territory, land, water and pasture, and differences in cultural outlook.

In response to the erratic rainfall distribution and resulting patchy vegetation, mobility has become the principal mode of resource use and production among the pastoral communities. In addition, pastoralists attempt to cope up with scarcity of pasture and other resources through managing diverse species of livestock, such as camels, goats, sheep, cattle and donkeys by taking advantage of the diverse natural resources and environmental variability (Helland 1980; Hogg 1997; Ayalew 2001; Getachew, 2000). However, as indicated above, competition over temporary patches of vegetation and water often entails conflicts with local communities around the patches.

Thus, a mobile mode of life, fragile ecology, climatic variability and the concomitant social structure call for livelihood policy and strategy compatible and feasible to changing pastoral systems (Workneh, 2006). It is premised that one of the important strategies of enhancing sustainable and dynamic livelihoods of pastoralists is through creating stronger economic and market interactions between lowland and highland economic systems.

Of course, there have been interactions between lowlanders and highlanders for centuries in terms of natural resource use, labor employment, trade and marketing, and technologies like farm tools and farming techniques. There is also a trend of increased penetration of markets in pastoral economic life, and pastoralists are increasingly involved in marketing of livestock and livestock products to generate income to buy food and non-food items. The interactions between these two economic systems, however, have been taking place in the bounds of conflicts of various scales.

It is generally true that market penetration into pastoral systems would create conditions for better market linkages with highland producers and traders and their economy. Moreover, entry into the market system would bring new opportunities for pastoralists to invest in non-pastoral resources and activities and open up ways and opportunities for wealth differentiation (Workneh, *et al.,* 2009). However, the nature, scope and constraints of economic and market interactions between lowland and highland systems and their potential roles in mitigating conflicts and in enhancing sustainable and growing pastoral livelihoods are not well studied.

This study was, therefore, aimed at investigating and understanding the nature, scope and constraints of economic and market interactions between lowland and highland economic systems and the implications of the interactions for sustainable livelihoods of pastoralists. The study focused specifically on examining the profile of pastoralists' economic engagements and their income contributions; exploring types and magnitude of product and service exchanges between lowland pastoralists and highland farmers and accessibility conditions of the major markets visited by pastoralists; assessing constraints to market interactions between lowland and highland communities; exploring the existing lowland pastoral and highland farming systems. The study has also attempted to draw implications of the lowland and highland economic interactions for mitigation of conflicts and pastoral economic growth.

2 Overview of Empirical Literature on Highland-lowland Economic Interactions

2.1 Market linkages between pastoralists and highland economic systems

Since livestock are considered as a means of wealth accumulation and indicators of social status in the societal hierarchy of pastoral systems, livestock sales decisions usually depend on family needs for cash to expend. The major expenditures of pastoral households are food items, medical care, stimulants and beverages, gifts, clothes, veterinary service and education (Kejela *et al.*, 2006).

Cattle are usually supplied by pastoralists and agro-pastoralists both to rural and urban markets in the highlands for use as source of beef and draught power by highlanders (PFE, 2004). In addition, pastoralists supply charcoal and firewood and to a slight degree milk and butter to markets to generate income. The other marketing linkage between the two production system is the flow of shoats to the export abattoirs, which are located at Debrezeit (Bishoftu), Modjo and Metahara towns along the Addis Ababa-Harar road axis (PFE, 2004).These abattoirs, despite their limited number and spatial distribution, serve as sustainable, reliable and organized market outlets for pastoralists.

Livestock marketing structure

There are three livestock marketing outlets in the country: the domestic channel, the formal live animal and meat export channel and the informal cross-border live animal trade (Getachew *et al.*, 2008). Based on their structure, the livestock markets found in Ethiopia can be categorized into four tiers; namely bush (farm gate), primary, secondary, and terminal markets (PFE, 2004). Primary markets are those in which the main sellers are producers and the main buyers are local assemblers and the number of animals that attend the market per market day is less than 500 heads.

In the secondary markets, the main sellers are local assemblers and main buyers are big traders, and the number of animals that attend the market is estimated between 500-1000 heads. In terminal markets, the main sellers are traders and main buyers are butcheries and restaurants and here more than 1000 heads of animals attend the market per day (Getachew *et al.*, 2008). Availability of elaborated market structure and diverse outlets are expected to facilitate pastoralists' interactions with the highland economic system.

In assessing live animal and meat export value chains in Ethiopia, Getachew *et al.* (2008) identified the following major livestock sources and market centers: Borena zone, Bale lowlands, Wollo area, Metehara and Miesso market centers and the Babile market in East Hararghe zone. A brief description of each of these is in order.

Borena zone is known for its high population of cattle, goat, camel and sheep in their orders of availability. It is also an important livestock supply area for live animal buyers and meat exporters. In this zone, there are 13 livestock markets of different sizes each connected with trucking/trekking routes. Even though most traders believe the price differential is rewarding for the inward movement of animals, the infrastructure problems in the area are perceived to encourage informal cross-border animal trade movements. The other challenge is the frequent clan conflicts, which influence the number of animals brought to the market.

Bale lowlands are also considered as sources of supply for cattle for both domestic and export markets. The major destinations for Bale cattle are Bale Robe and its surrounding areas, Hararghe highlands, Dera and Adama. It is reported that Bale Robe and the neighboring highlanders use relatively aged Borana breed cows for slaughter purposes. The Harerghe highlands are other domestic markets for Bale cattle. Young bulls are bought by traders who come from Hararghe to Melka-Oda and Seweina markets in the Bale lowlands. These animals are trekked for about eight days to Hararghe and sold to farmers to be used as draught animals for some time and for fattening later on. Borana breed cattle are also trekked to Dera and Adama to be fattened for three months and sold at the Addis Ababa market for domestic consumption. The export market also absorbs young bulls trekked from this area to Adama via Dera. Camels from Bale lowlands are also transported to Miesso usually by trucks. They are then exported to the Egyptian market via the Port of Djibouti (Getachew *et al.* (2008).

Wollo is one of the sources of exportable shoat and cattle as reported by the same study. The most important livestock markets in this case are Kemiesse, Habru, Bati, Degan, Kombolcha, Senbete and Bora. These markets are located in the semi-pastoralist areas where farmers are engaged in both crop and livestock production. Shoats from the Afar areas reach these markets through numerous small traders operating in the area. Bati, the largest livestock market in Wollo attracts pastoralists from as far away as four days round-trip distance. Cattle from this market are also used for draught purpose. On the other hand, the Raya Azebo breed cattle sourced from Kemiesse market are also used as live animal export. Small traders use trucks to transport cattle form southern Wollo to the Adama feedlots for the domestic market. In addition, shoats collected from this area are used by export abattoirs or live animal exporters.

Metehara and Miesso markets are also important market sources for exportable livestock in Central Rift Valley. On the other hand, Metehara is a secondary market where small traders bring shoats from Afar and the surrounding primary markets. Abattoirs and live animal exporters do buy considerable number of animals also from this market.

Miesso market is also a secondary market that sourced livestock from the surrounding primary livestock markets, such as Bedesa, Chiro, Hirna, Beroda, Asebot, Kora and other markets in the neighboring Somali lowlands. Frequent conflicts between Somali and Oromo pastoralists are problems that constrain livestock marketing in the area.

Babile, located in East Hararghe Zone, is a big livestock market where all types of livestock are traded. This market serves both the formal and informal export channels. The formal (legal) export channel is the live animal export trade via Togwajale and Djibouti. Babile market also supplies significant number of shoats to the export abattoirs. The informal export channel is the smuggling of cattle and shoats through the Ethio-Somalia border to different countries. Babile market is characterized by clan-based marketing systems where Somali pastoralists take their animals in group and operate the transaction facilitated by brokers from their own clan.

2.2 Challenges and constraints to participation in the market

Generally, due to low population densities, remoteness and high transport costs, pastoralists have poor access to markets. Getachew *et.al.* (2008) classified livestock marketing constraints into two broad categories – infrastructural and non-infrastructural factors. A brief discussion is in order.

Challenges related to market infrastructure

Road network: Road plays a crucial role in livestock marketing systems. The type of road connecting of an area determines the type of buyers that can get access to its market and also the profitability of the participants in the market. In this regard, Getachew *et.al* (2008) compared markets located in Borena and the Bale lowlands. In Borena, the most important livestock markets like Dubuluq, Mega and Harobeke, are located on the asphalt road that stretches from Addis

Ababa to Moyale; and this has helped exporters to easily transport animals to quarantines or abattoirs at relatively lower cost. However, because the Bale lowlands are connected to the center of the country by very rough gravel road, it is very difficult to frequently penetrate and transport livestock for the export market. Due to this, truck owners charge exorbitant prices to load animals from such areas. As a result, traders and abattoirs often give priority to other supply sources.

High cost and poor transport service: Due to the poor state of transportation, pastoralists incur high costs when they take animals to the market. The study of pastoralist livestock marketing behavior in Ethiopia and Kenya by Osterloh *et al.* (2003) pointed out that 67% of Kenyan and 79% of Ethiopian pastoralists incur some sort of cash cost in their livestock transaction, though the percentage of the incurred fees greatly varies from one area to the other.

In addition to the transportation costs borne for trekking or trucking of animals, pastoralists incur expenses as they move from one place to another in search of water and pasture. In both Kenya and Ethiopia, average costs of human transportation exceed those of transporting the animals to the market. The sum of animals and human transport costs comprises the largest component of marketing costs in both Ethiopia and Kenya, scaling up to 44% and 60%, respectively (Osterloh *et al.* 2003).

Market Information System: A market information system is needed to disseminate up-to-date market information such as price, time specific demands and quality information to all livestock market participants. Information is not equally shared among the different actors and stakeholders. As a result, there have been some efforts to develop an information system by various organizations such as the Livestock Marketing Authority of the then MoARD and the USAID supported project called LINKS. The problem is, however, that the developed systems were not able to reach the producers at the right time and in a form that is easily understandable. This situation results often in unpredictable quantity and quality of products destined for internal and export markets and less remunerative prices for producers. It also limits the development of value addition by various participants, such as producers, traders and processors (Getachew *et al.*, 2008).

Communication infrastructures: Access to communication infrastructures like telephone would help households to access information easily and reduce transaction costs significantly. For instance, the availability and use of mobile phones by northern traders in Nairobi makes it easy to communicate to their partners in Moyale about current market conditions before making purchase decisions (Mahmoud 2003 cited in Osterloh *et al.* (2003). There is also significant change in the use of mobile communication technology. For instance, there are field level evidences to show that pastoralists in the Borena area are already making best use of cell phones to gather information on prices as well as connect with suppliers inside the country as well as across the border.

Non-infrastructural challenges

Drought: Drought is a recurrent climatic phenomenon in pastoral areas of lowland Ethiopia. Drought has a prolonged effect on pastoral production systems by disrupting the food supply condition, income source, social norms and terms of trade. These effects, in turn, erode the economic resilience of pastoralists and aggravate their vulnerability.

The study conducted by UN OCHA- PCI (2007) shows the challenges associated with livestock trade and drought in the Somali region of Ethiopia. According to the study, Gode, Shinile and Gashamo *woredas* of the region were identified to have received the worst hit of the 1999-2000, 2002 and 2004 drought that struck the region respectively. These phenomena weakened and reduced the demand for livestock in Gode and Gashamo markets in the respective years. Prices of livestock collapsed as low as US$ 1.53 (13 *Birr*) for a grown sheep, meaning that the entire sheep was then only as valuable as its skin.

Drought is also associated with the collapse of the health of livestock and decline in the barter terms of trade, i.e. livestock to grain prices. For example, in the Somali region, there was a temporary collapse of the market in Gashamo *woreda* in 2004 due to the drought. The lack of forage caused animals to become weak and lose weight, which greatly reduced their marketability and led to the collapse of livestock market by the second half of 2004. Even for the ones that were available in the market, the terms of trade were not favorable and a grown sheep could no longer exchange for the 50 kilo sack of food (IDS, 2006).

A study conducted by Fasil *et al* (2001) in Afar and Borana areas also showed the significant impact of drought on the livestock population. Their findings in Afar revealed that livestock populations had decreased by 50%; while livestock prices had become very low. Moreover, gain prices had become extremely expensive. For example, the 1983/85 drought in Borana led to 60% decrease due to mortality, slaughter and sales in sample herds over two years. Similarly, the 1995-97 drought led to 78% decrease in cattle herd size and 45% decrease in camel herd size among sampled households in the Somali and Borana areas (Fasil *et al.*, 2001).

Trade bans: The biggest and most lucrative livestock market for the Horn of Africa is the Middle East, especially the Kingdom of Saudi Arabia, which imports literally millions of sheep, goats and cattle every year. The horn of

Africa has traditionally been the primary source for this market (IDS, 2006; UN OCHA-PCI, 2007). East African access to this market has however been severely disrupted twice by the imposition of a ban on livestock imports in the last ten years. The ban was imposed because of an outbreak of Rift Valley fever in East Africa, which caused widespread livestock mortality, especially of sheep. But its effects on trade were much more significant than the mortality itself, leading to sharp decline in livestock prices throughout the region and traders in the Somali region of Ethiopia stopping buying animals. In the rural markets, demand went down as those who fatten and prepare the animals for resale to export traders ceased buying (UN OCHA-PCI, 2007; IDS, 2006).

Lack of livestock extension service: In most areas, where major livestock markets are available, the agricultural extension system is not as such active to provide appropriate support to producers about production of livestock for the market. For instance, pastoralist and rural development agents in Bale, South Wollo and Kemiesse were found to have weak communication with livestock markets supplying to the export market (Getachew *et al.*, 2008). Market-focused livestock extension service is needed in order to assist farmers and pastoralists produce quality livestock required in the market. It can also help in improving the marketing behavior, which is important for sustainable supply to the markets.

Conflicts: Due to increased population pressure, drought and other factors in both lowland and highland production systems, there is an increasing competition over the control and use of scarce resources like land and water sources. This and other related historical and cultural factors have led to numerous conflicts in different parts of the country. According to Getachew *et. al* (2008), whenever there is clan conflict in Borana area, the market is disrupted and the number of animals brought to the export abattoirs decreases significantly. To determine the association between conflicts and livestock supply, they compared livestock transaction records that took place in the area when there was and there was no clan conflict in the area. Their findings show that at times of conflict there was a substantial supply shortage reaching as low as 50% compared to that in the normal period.

Studies conducted by Muluken (2009) and Akmel (2010) in the northeastern part of the country show that whenever Amhara and Afar ethnic groups are involved in conflict, the number of Afar, especially males, that visit the livestock market centers located in the highlands of Amhara region decreases significantly. The situation makes traders insecure and markets to be unreliable supply sources.

Policy and institutional issues

For the last several decades, the pastoralist areas have been marginalized in terms of socio-economic development. The country's policies, strategies and programs have overlooked pastoralists' way of life and living conditions, and until recently, they have experienced socio-political exclusion. Because of all these factors, pastoralists remained the poorest of the poor and became more vulnerable to a growing process of impoverishment (MoFED, 2005)

Institutionally, the major policy steps implemented so far by the government to integrate pastoralist economies into the national economy include insuring the constitutional rights of pastoralists not to be displaced from their own land, devolution of power to regions and hence *woredas* and formation of pastoral institutions, including a Pastoral Affairs Standing Committee in the parliament, a national Pastoral Community Development Program (PCDP) and a Pastoralist Area Development Department (PADD) and Inter-Ministerial Board under the Ministry of Federal Affairs. The pastoral areas extension team and pastoral development coordination team within MoARD are responsible for providing institutional support for the pastoral regions as well. In addition, the pastoral regional states have reformulated many of their institutions to incorporate pastoralism in their planning processes.

In the process of diversifying livelihood systems, the market plays a pivotal role. Without the mechanism to develop the market in place, individuals with the potential to be entrepreneurs cannot move on to different forms of livelihood (PFE, 2004). The government emphasized in its policies and strategies the role of markets in tackling the different socioeconomic challenges. For instance, various rural development policies and strategies state that agricultural development will not be rapid and sustainable unless it is market oriented. In connection with this policy, the government encourages the development of an agricultural sector that produces for the market and establishment of an efficient market system that enables producers to maintain the quality and competitiveness of agricultural products.

The Ethiopian government Plan for Accelerated and Sustained Development to End Poverty (PASDEP) points out that the terms of trade between livestock and cereals has often become unbearable for pastoralists during dry seasons. Besides, the existing inefficient livestock marketing system aggravates pastoral food insecurity. In this regard, PASDEP and the Food Security Strategy emphasize the importance of a marketing system that increases the off-take from herds, especially in pastoral areas, and marketing of dairy products. To deal with this objective, the government has designed strategies such as: facilitating local and cross-border livestock trading with better market information; establishment of micro-finance institutions tailored to conditions and contexts of pastoralists to support pastoral trading activities; promotion and certification of quarantine services; restoring the stocker/feeder program through private or livestock cooperatives; and, promotion of commercialization of livestock production (MoFED, 2005).

3   Conceptual Framework and Methodology

This section presents the conceptual framework of the study through which the pillars and components of the interactions of lowland and highland systems are examined. The section also discusses the research design and methods of data collection employed for the study.

3.1   Conceptual framework

The conceptual premise of the study is that economic interaction between pastoral and highland economic systems is influenced by multiple factors. These factors include production and productivity of the dominant economic activity of each economic system; availability of markets and market infrastructure; the social relationship among different socio-cultural groups in the economic systems; availability of comparative advantages that each system possesses; presence of institutions that enhance production and marketing activities of each economic system, and conflict mitigation efforts and change in cultural attitudes. Income status of the population in each economic system has also an important role in market interactions between the economic systems through its effect on economic demand. Market interactions, in turn, would have significant impact on mitigating conflicts among the interacting communities of the two economic systems. The inter-relationships of the various factors are depicted in Figure 1.

Figure 1: Conceptual framework of the factors that affect the lowland-highland
market interactions

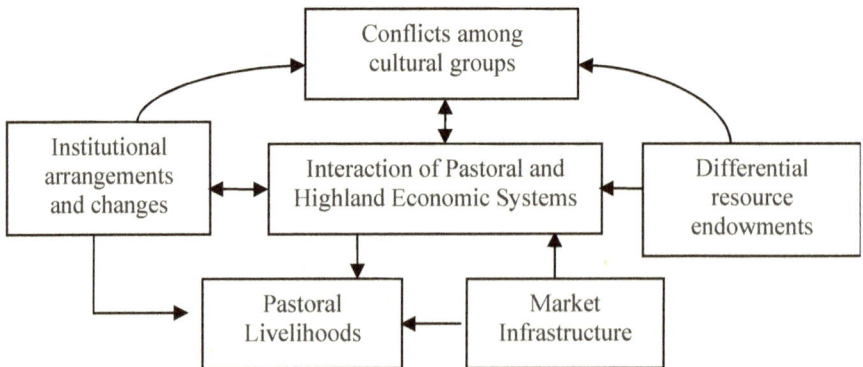

As pointed out earlier, the pastoral economic system is located geographically in lowland areas and its major economic activity is based up on livestock production often in mobile and/or semi-mobile systems. The highland economy, on the other hand, is dominated by sedentary mixed farming, producing mainly crops with some livestock. The pastoral economic system mainly supplies livestock and livestock products to the market while the highland economic system supplies mainly crop products and non-crop food and non-food goods as well as services. The interactions of both systems in terms of exchange of goods and services would be to the benefit of both systems, and particularly to the pastoral systems, whose development status is relatively low in all aspects. Such interactions create conducive condition for better access of pastoralists to various social services such as health and education, and help the development of harmonious social relations.

While interactions of both systems influence indirectly the expansion of market infrastructure and institutions, institutions themselves are also important for the enhancement of multifarious interactions of pastoral and highland economic systems. Improved livelihood sources are often accompanied by better income that indirectly creates demand for goods and services from highland economic systems. Furthermore, the traditional and long-standing conflicts among pastoralists and highland communities would cease to be bottlenecks. This would further pave the way for the expansion of the interaction of the two systems which would also play important role in curbing conflicts among different cultural groups.

3.2   Methodology

The case study was conducted in two purposively selected *woredas* (districts) on the basis of cross-sectional quantitative and qualitative data. The quantitative data were gathered through household surveys, while qualitative data were gathered from different actors using different techniques, including key informant interviews and observations.

3.2.1   Study sites

The study sites selected for the study are Semurobi-na-Gelealo (SRG) *woreda* and Dulecha *woreda* located in zone five and zone three of the Afar Regional State respectively. Both *woredas* are predominantly inhabited by the Afar ethnic group with limited presence of people from other ethnic groups. Both *woredas* are adjacent to highland *woredas* of northeastern Amhara Regional State and are connected to the highland economic systems through lowland-highland interfacing areas or corridors (Figure 2 and 3). These pastoral *woredas* were

13

selected purposively as they are considered to depict the pastoral livelihoods and their interactions with the highlands are more evident.

SRG *woreda* and its neighboring *woredas* are connected to Kewot and its surrounding highland *woredas* through the Shewarobit town and its vicinities. Kumame, the capital town of SRG, is about 45 kms. away from Shewarobit, the capital town of Kewot *woreda*. Climatically, SRG is semi-arid with low rainfall and poor water resource. The part of the Kewot *woreda* towards Kumame is lowland and its mid-altitude is inhabited mainly by members of the Amhara ethnic group mingled with some families of Argoba ethnic origin engaged in agriculture. Areas of Kewot *woreda* past Shewarobit towards west are highlands inhabited by farmers from the Amhara ethnic group. Kewot *woreda* is adjacent in its northern side with Senbete area, which is part of the Oromia zone in Amhara region.

Dulecha *woreda* and its neighboring Afar *woredas* are connected with the Ankober highland and its neighboring highland *woredas* through Gachine town of Argoba Liyu *woreda* and Aliyuamba, emerging town within Ankober *woreda*. It is also connected with Awash Sebat within Zone Three of the Afar region. All the roads connecting to these neighboring *woredas*, except Awash Sebat, are poor and pose considerable difficulty particularly during rainy seasons. This is not the part of the study *woredas* but is an important pathway or area lying between highland Ankober and the pastoral lowlands. Another section of Argoba Liyu *woreda* connects with SRG *woreda* at its south eastern corner. It is lowland inhabited dominantly by agro-pastoralists of people of Argoba ethnic origin. The Argoba community is sometimes involved in conflicts with Amhara communities as well as with the Afar mainly due to competition over scarce water and pasture resources. Discussions were held, however, with three key informants (experts and administrators) at Gachine town to get their views about the interactions among Argoba, Amhara and Afar communities.

The highland *woredas* sub-adjacent to the selected pastoral *woredas* are inhabited predominantly by members of the Amhara ethnic group, while the population inhabiting the towns of Kewot and Shewarobit are mixed populations, such as the Oromos, Gurages and Tigrians.

Figure 2: Map of the highland and lowland study *woredas*

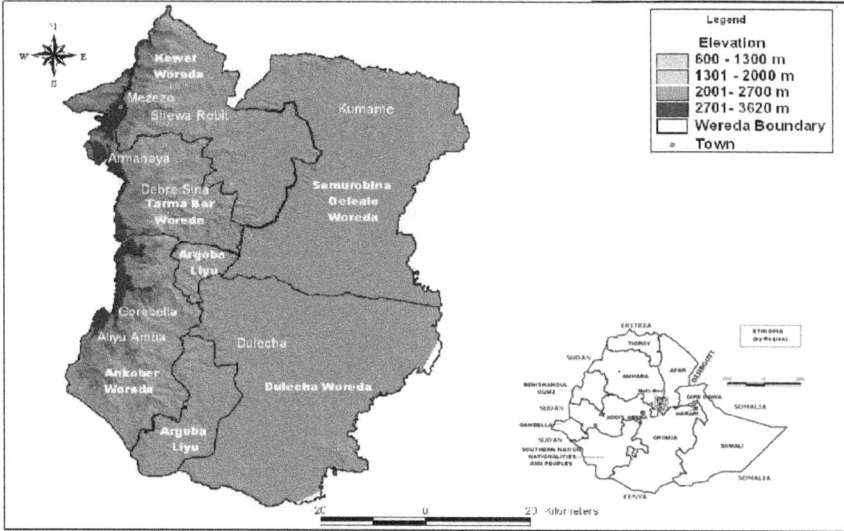

Figure 3: Map of the Study sites

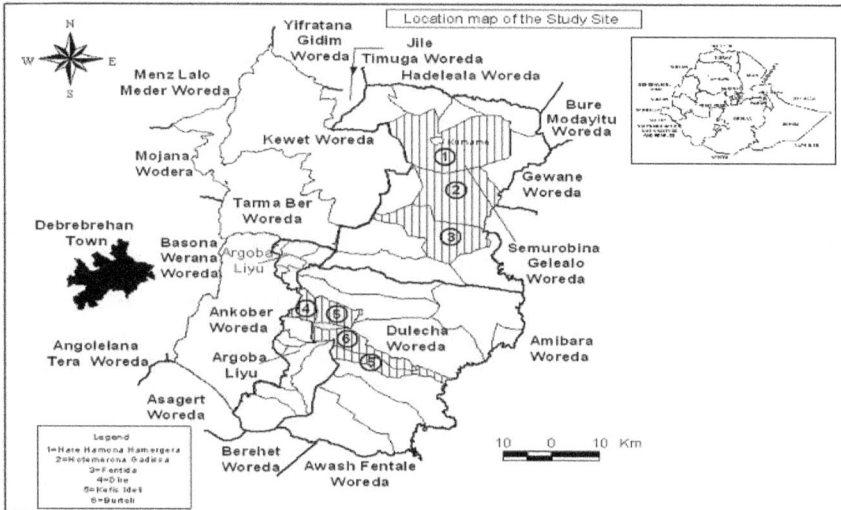

3.2.2   Data collection methods

Two data sources were used for this study- primary and secondary. Primary sources were used to get data on issues related to economic interactions and market linkages, pastoral livelihoods, conflict situations and institutional arrangements that link lowland and highland systems and were collected directly from pastoral households residing in the sites, development workers and experts working in the areas. Secondary sources included reports and statistical abstracts. Household surveys were not conducted on highland farm households because of the short time period for the study and limited resources to accomplish the task. However, in-depth case farmer interviews and key informant interviews were done with highland farmers, development agents and experts working in the highland economic system. For any similar future studies, gathering survey data from highland farmers would be useful to get quantitative data about their economic linkages and perceptions of the interactions with pastoralists.

In Summary, the following data collection methods were employed to collect the data:

(i) **Sample household survey**: A household survey was conducted to collect data from a total of 80 sample households, forty from each *woreda*. In each *woreda*, forty pastoral households were selected from three purposively selected *kebeles,* one *kebele* located nearer to town and the other two *kebeles* relatively far from the center. The *kebeles* selected from SRG are (1) Harehamo-na-Hamergera (2) Hotemero-na-Gadsiisa and (3) Fentida, while those of Dulecha *woreda* are (1) Burteli (2) Kefis Ideli and (3) Dire. The small sample size taken in each woreda is considered to represent the more or less homogenous community in each *woreda* in terms of livelihood activities and culture and mode of interactions and relationships with neighboring highland systems. The households were selected randomly from each of the three *kebeles*, 13 households from each of the two *kebeles*, and 14 from the remaining one *kebele.* Unwilling and unavailable households were substituted by willing and available neighboring households with facilitation support from the chairman of each *kebele.* As can be seen in Table 2, 12.5% of the total sample households are female headed households.

Table 2: Size of sample households by study *woreda* (site)

Sample size	SRG	Dulecha	Total
Male	37 (92.5 %)	33 (82.5%)	70 (87.5%)
Female	3 (7.55)	7 (17.5%)	10 (12.5%)
Total	40 (100%)	40 (100%)	80 100%)

SOURCE: Own survey, August 2010

(ii) **Focus Group Discussion**: Focus group discussions (FGDs) were conducted in each *woreda* to gather views and perceptions about the economic interactions between the lowland and the highland economies. Each focus group consisted of six pastoralists, two from each sample *Kebele* and one or two of them being women. The FGD in each *woreda* was conducted in *woreda* towns, which is the central place pastoralists prefer to come to. The discussion in each *woreda* took about two and half hours.

(iii) **In-depth case interviews**: In each *woreda*, in-depth interviews were conducted with three randomly selected household heads using a pre-prepared checklist. The case households were selected in consultation with the development agent, the supervisor and the *woreda* pastoral development officer and administrator. The selected pastoralists and farmers were found to be willing and knowledgeable about the area and able to speak about his/her livelihood activities and views on the interactions between pastoralists and the highland economic system. In each *woreda*, one of the in-depth case pastoralists is a woman. Similarly, in-depth interviews were also conducted with three case farm household heads in neighboring highland *kebeles* interfacing with the pastoral study sites. The in-depth case interviews generated information about the individual's livelihood situation and activities, his/her interactions with highland economic systems, challenges faced and his/her views on the importance of the interactions

(iv) **Key informants interview**: Interviews were conducted with eight informants in each site. The list included experts from highland *woreda* Agricultural and Rural Development Offices, *woreda* Pastoral, Agricultural and Rural Development Offices, Officers of *Woreda* Conflict Prevention and Resolution Offices in Kewot *woreda* and Ankober *woreda*, the Farm Africa officer in SRG *woreda* and the Action Aid officer in Ankober *woreda*, administration officers and experts in Dulecha pastoral *woreda* and Argoba-Liyu *woreda*. The checklist that describes the content of the inquiry is given in Annex 3.

(v) **Observation**: The researcher observed three market places in each *woreda*, taking about one hour for each market. In the course of the observation, important parameters, such as size of participants, types of goods supplied and whereabouts of the rural and urban participants and their occupations were considered. Observation also helped to critically scrutinize the substantial topographic, social, and agro-climatic variations between the two economic regions.

(vi) **Secondary data**: Secondary data were also collected from study reports, maps, reports of Ministry of Federal Affairs and CSA statistical abstracts.

3.2.3   Data analysis

The household survey data were analyzed employing descriptive statistics, such as mean, maximum, minimum and percentages. Data gathered through FGD, in-depth case interviews and key informants interviews were summarized thematically and analyzed qualitatively in terms of narrations so as to provide insights on the research issues.

4   Characteristics and Livelihood Profile of Study Households

This section describes the demographic and socio-economic characteristics of the sample households and presents discussions and findings related to the livelihood systems of the pastoralists. It addresses the different components of livelihood systems of the pastoralists/agro-pastoralists in the study *woredas* on the basis of the survey data and qualitative information gathered through FGD, KII and in-depth case studies. The section focuses on the strategies and activities of the livelihood system and the effects that the interaction of pastoral and highland economic systems produce on secure and sustainable livelihoods.

4.1   Demographic and socioeconomic characteristics of sample households

As shown in Table 3, the average age for sample household heads in SRG *woreda* is 33, while that of Dulecha *woreda* is 41, both falling relatively within young family groups. Young pastoral family heads often have desires to move to different places and to work hard to improve their livelihoods. The average family size of the sample households in both study *woreda* is 8 with almost equal number of male and female members. The minimum and maximum number of family sizes in both *woredas*, SRG and Dulecha *woreda*, is 3 and 18 respectively. A large family size often means large labor resource, which is needed for extensive and mobile livestock production and market interaction.

Table 3: Demographic characteristics of sample households

Item	SRG	Dulecha	Both *woredas*
Age			
Mean	33.56	41	37.28
Min	20	25	20
Max	60	70	70
N	40	40	80
Family size			
Mean	8.07	8.18	8.13
Min.	3.00	3.00	3.00
Max.	15	18.0	18
N	40	40	80
Children ($\leq$14)			
Male	2.90	2.33	2.61
Female	2.13	2.13	2.13
Adults ($\geq$15)			
Male	1.20	1.78	1.49
Female	1.85	1.95	1.90

SOURCE: Own survey, August 2010

Education level of sample household heads

The majority of heads of the sample households in both Dulecha *woreda* (95%) and SRG *woreda* (62.2%) are non-literate (Table 4). However, in relative terms, pastoralists in the SRG *woreda* are better educated compared to that in Dulecha *woreda*.

Table 4: Education level of sample households in the study *kebeles*

Level of Education	SRG		Dulecha		Total	
	Frequency	Percent	Frequency	Percent	Frequency	Percent
Non-literate	25	62.5	38	95.0	63	78.75
1 - 4 grades	4	10	2	5	6	7.5
5 - 8 grades	8	20	-	-	8	10.0
9 - 10 grades	3	7.5	-	-	3	3.75
Total	40	100	40	100	80	100

SOURCE: Own survey, August 2010

Livestock resource

Livestock is the major resource base upon which the livelihoods of pastoralists are dependent. The four major livestock categories held by the pastoral households in all the study *kebeles* are goat, cattle, sheep and camel, in that order. Size of livestock holdings of the sample households is given in Table 5.

Since livestock production is the major source of livelihood of pastoralists, larger numbers of livestock imply better livelihood, particularly in the context where improved breeds and adequate quality feed and management practices are uncommon.

Table 5: Average livestock holdings of sample households

Item	SRG (N=40)	Dulecha (N=40)	Both *woredas* (N=80)
Oxen	0.78	0.60	0.69
Cow	5.18	4.93	5.05
Young bulls	0.93	0.43	0.68
Heifer	1.08	0.93	1.00
Calves	2.20	1.35	1.78
Sheep	8.75	8.88	8.81
Goat	21.08	17.98	19.52
Horse	0.00	0.00	0.00
Donkey	1.43	1.13	1.27

Mule	0.03	0.03	0.03
Camel	5.13	3.70	4.41
Poultry	0.35	1.25	0.80
Total	3.91	3.43	3.67

SOURCE: Own survey, August 2010

Access to finance

Finance for pastoralists is crucial because most of them are now increasingly dependent on food grains and other consumables from highland or lowland markets. Financial resource is therefore an important factor that enhances economic and market linkages of pastoralists with the highland economy. However, saving and credit experience of the sample households was found to be negligible. Only three pastoralists (One from SRG and two from Dulecha *woreda*) (3.8%) were involved in micro-credit institutions and have accumulated some saving at micro finance institutions. No pastoralist reported membership in informal saving and credit institution such as *Iqub*. Similarly, only two sampled pastoralists in SRG *woreda* and one sampled pastoralist in Dulecha *woreda* have saving in formal banks. In each study site, only one pastoralist (2.5%) reported that he received some remittance and the remaining did not obtain any remittance from other sources.

Land holding and soil quality

It is a common knowledge that pastoralists do not often hold arable land of their own except homesteads, while agro-pastoralists do hold land that they cultivate. Table 6 shows the size of land holding and cultivated land during the survey year, 2010 cropping year. As shown in Table 6, 42.5% of sample households in SRG *woreda* and 22.5% in Dulecha *woreda* did not have their own farmland. There are more of agro-pastoralists in Dulecha *woreda* sample than in SRG *woreda* sample. The average area of arable land held by the sample households was 0.82 ha. and 1.06 ha in SRG and Dulecha *woreda* respectively. Given large tract of land available in pastoral areas, the average arable land seems to be higher than the national average, which is below one hectare. Here, the major constraint of agricultural production is lack or shortage of rainfall and the less fertility of the soil. Share cropping/renting is a rare practice in both study areas. Only four pastoralists/agro-pastoralists rented-in/sharecropped-in farmlands from others in Dulecha site during the survey year. None has done so in SRG site. Similarly, only two agro-pastoralists/pastoralists in each site rented-out/share-cropped out land, mainly to relatives. This limited informal land access

21

arrangement practice could be related, inter alia, to poor economic linkage the pastoralists have with highland farmers, who could have rented–in/ or shared-in land from pastoralists.

The pastoralists were asked to indicate the rate of fertility of their arable land according to their observation. Accordingly, 68.2% of the respondents in SRG sample and 81.6% of the sample respondents in Dulecha indicated that the fertility of their arable land was good. This fertility status matches with the situation that most of the pastoralists in Dulecha sample are engaged in farming compared with that in SRG sample.

Similarly, pastoralists who hold their own grazing land are limited in number. As shown in Table 6, 77.5% and 82.5% of SRG and Dulecha sample households respectively did not have their own grazing land. The average size of grazing land owned by pastoralists in SRG and Dulecha sample households are 0.95 ha and 0.40 ha respectively. The data on soil fertility and soil quality point out the decisions of the pastoralists and agro-pastoralists on their land use pattern. Pastoralists who evaluate their soil to be fertile (e.g. in Dulecha area) go for agro-pastoral activities, while sites (e.g. SRG area) endowed with relatively larger grazing land focus on livestock rearing.

Table 6: Size of landholdings (ha.) and soil fertility of sample households, 2009
SOURCE: Own survey, August 2010

Item	SRG (N=40)	Dulecha (N=40)	Both *woredas* (N=80)
Landless	17 (42.5%)	9 (22.5%)	26 (32.5%)
Own land holding			
Mean	1.7938	1.5063	1.6500
Min	0.0000	0.0000	0.0000
Max	7.0000	8.0000	8.0000
Arable landless	19 (47.5%)	12 (30%)	31 (38.8%)
Owned arable land			
Mean	0.8188	1.0563	0.9375
Min.	0.00	0.00	0.00
Max.	4.00	4.25	4.25
Grazing landless	31 (77.5%)	33 (82.5%)	64 (80%)
Own grazing land			
Mean	0.9500	0.4000	0.6750
Min	0.0000	0.0000	0.0000
Max	6.0000	6.0000	6.0000
Soil fertility, status			
Fertile	15 (68.2%)	26 (81.6%)	41 41 (75.9%)
Medium	7 (31.8%)	2 3 (9.4%)	10 (18.5%)
Poor	-	3 3 (9.4%)	2 3 (5.6%)

4.2 Livelihood strategies and activities

Livestock production is the key source of livelihoods of pastoralists while production of cereals, combined with livestock, is the major source of livelihood for agro-pastoralists. As observed from the survey, the main crops grown by pastoralists in SRG are *Masho* (mungbean), maize, sorghum, haricot bean, *teff* and red pepper. *Masho* and maize were grown by 16 agro-pastoralists, while five pastoralists produce sorghum and each of the remaining crops was grown only by a single agro-pastoralist. *Masho* was grown on average on 0.82, while maize and sorghum were grown on 0.71 and 0.80 hectares on average respectively.

Similarly, the major crops grown by Dulecha *woreda* sample agro-pastoralists were sorghum, maize and *teff*. Sorghum was grown by 20 agro-pastoralists

(50%), while maize and *teff* were grown by 18 (45%) and 3 (7.5%) agro-pastoralists respectively. Onion, tomato and red pepper were each grown by two agro-pastoralists, while a pastoral household grew banana. The average areas allocated for sorghum, maize and *teff* by the growers in Dulecha area were 1.16 0.83 and 0.42 hectares respectively. While *Masho* and maize are relatively common in SRG, sorghum and maize are dominant in Dulecha area in terms of both area coverage and number of growers. In addition, while *Masho* and red pepper serve as cash crops, the remaining crops are predominantly cultivated for household consumption.

Discussion with various key informants, including Pastoral, Agricultural and Rural Development Office experts and officers of SRG *woreda* as well as experts from some NGOs in the *woreda* such as Farm Africa, revealed that the major source of livelihoods of the people in the *woreda* is livestock farming and petty trading. Currently, out of the twelve *kebeles* of the *woreda*, six *kebeles* are involved in irrigated crop farming. Two *kebeles* (Kedebora and Ade Elli-Hingig) are engaged in irrigated crop farming. In the *woreda*, the major income portion of pastoralists comes from goat farming followed by camel and cattle in their order of importance. They also get milk from camel, cattle and goat in that order, especially when there is good rainfall. Some pastoralists produce and sell butter; however, the milk production is not often large enough to supply to markets. As observed by a key informant, crop farming is also becoming a useful source of income for many of the pastoralists in SRG *woreda*.

With regard to constraints to animal production, some key informants pointed out that animal production in the area is hindered by water and pasture shortage. Animal diseases are also a significant problem, particularly during the drought seasons. Easy movement and access to grazing land is often constrained by recurrent conflict between the lowlanders and highland communities.

Besides livestock and crop production, pastoralists and agro-pastoralists do get income from non-farm and off-farm activities, such as fire wood collection, petty trading and small businesses.

The household survey has generated data on gross income of the sample households from different sources. As shown in the Table 7, all the sample households in SRG and Dulecha obtained income from livestock sales. The income obtained from sale of livestock was the highest compared to other sources, such as grain, horticultural crops, animal products and off-/non-farm sources. The average income obtained by a sample household in SRG and Dulecha is *Birr* 8488.75 and 5680.90 respectively. Ten households out of forty in each of SRG and Dulecha sites were involved in off-/non-farm income activities. A pastoralist who participated in off-/non-farm activities in SRG got an average annual income of 2,547 *Birr*, while a pastoralist in Dulecha got an average of 2,172 *Birr*.

Participation in sale of livestock products provides a very important source of income for a considerable number of pastoralists (35%) in Dulecha. Only two sample households in SRG reported to have participated in livestock product sales. The results point out that livestock sales, off-/non-farm and livestock product sales are important sources of income for pastoralists and agro-pastoralists. Dulecha sample households get lower income from livestock sales relative to SRG pastoralists. This could be related to the situation that Dulecha pastoralists get their food to some extent from own crop production, while SRG pastoralists have to sell more of livestock to buy food.

Table 7: Gross annual income of households by sources of income in Birr, 2009/10

Woreda	Item	Sources of income				
		Grain crops	Horticultural Crops	Live animals	Animal products	Off/Non-farm Activities
SRG	Minimum	2,200	.	600	18	300
	Maximum	2,200	.	21,500	832	6,000
	Mean	2,200	.	8489	425	2,547
	Valid N	N=1	N=0	N=40	N=2	N=10
Dulecha	Minimum	4,500	1,090	405	40	450
	Maximum	4,500	4,300	14,480	3440	4,200
	Mean	4,500	3,130	5,681	1073	2,172
	Valid N	N=1	N=3	N=39	N=14	N=10

SOURCE: Own household survey, August 2010

The common off-farm income source for pastoralists and agro-pastoralists is firewood collection and charcoal production. Tree cutting, which has been a taboo for a long time, is now being breached by many Afar people to make way for charcoal production and sale to traders or consumers. As reported by key informants and experts in Dulecha *woreda*, however, the main economic engagement of the people of Dulecha *woreda* is pastoralism (87.5%), while about 12.5% of them are engaged in agro-pastoralism. Agro-pastoralists in one of the *kebeles* of Dulecha (Dire *kebele*) are engaged, for example, in sedentary crop farming on irrigation and rainfall basis.

The major livestock types kept in Dulecha are goat and sheep followed by cattle and camel. Recently, the number of animals in the *woreda* has been declining mainly because of diminishing access to pasture and water and diseases problems. The pastoralists in the *woreda* practice seasonal migration in search of pasture and water in neighboring *woredas*, such as Argoba (Tachmeteklia *kebele*), Amibara and Ankober, and Sabure in the Awash Valley.

According to key informants and experts, extensive livestock framing is under threat due to desertification and declining rainfall and grazing land. Pastoralists are shifting from large animals, such as cattle and camels, to small ruminants, including goats and sheep. It was also pointed out that introducing large-scale rangeland improvement and irrigated crop farming programs would be instrumental to maintain livestock farming at a sustainable level. Fodder production on irrigation basis supplemented by multi-nutrition blocks could also be part of range improvement and feed management. The following narration of a pastoralist, Hamedo Hassen, from SRG site sheds light on pastoral livelihood activities and situation presented above.

> *Ato Hamedo Hassen, aged 36, is a pastoralist living in a kebele around Kumame/SRG, with a family size of 12. He is non-literate. He has only about 20 goats and no other livestock. He cultivates about two timad of farmland when there is rainfall and good conditions. But rainfall often fails and diseases break out. He does not have a grazing land of his own. He grazes his animals on communal pasture land in nearby places during the rainfall period. During the dry period, he sends his animals with those of other neighboring pastoralists to remote pasture areas outside his woreda, mainly to a place called Alai Degi, in the direction of Gewani. For instance, last year, he sent his animals to this place, where the animals stayed for a long period, i.e. September to June. Goat farming is the primary income source for Hamedo family, followed by a salary he obtains from his service as chairperson of his kebele administration (300 birr/month). Although it is a bit exaggerated, he reported that he sells about 40 young goats per year, each with average price of 150 Birr (6,000 Birr per year). The third important economic activity is crop farming, which provides food for the household. He does not produce surplus for the market.*

Generally, in both *woredas*, livestock production is the major livelihood strategy with some supplemental role for non-/off-farm alternative. In situations where there is shortage of water and pasture and livestock disease is rampant, crop production as an alternative livelihood strategy is becoming important, though constrained by various problems.

4.3 Women's role in livelihood activities

Pastoral women do bear heavy responsibilities and duties in household activities and management. Women's activities and responsibilities include food preparation, taking care of children and small ruminants, fetching water and firewood, marketing, loading and unloading temporary house construction materials on the back of camels during movement to remote pasture areas, participating in house construction. The following narrative about a case of a woman household head demonstrates the livelihood situation of female headed households.

> *Mrs. Aguwa Aden, 30, non-literate with three children, is a divorced woman household head. Her fourth child died at the age of two. Her two children go to school. She has ten goats. Goat farming is the major source of income, followed by firewood collection and selling and trading, mainly honey and tobacco. The major problems that she faces include labor shortage to attend her goats and/or children, and shortage of water for her goats. She has no arable land to cultivate. She goes to Shewarobit market at least once a fortnight to sell her commodities and buy food grain such as wheat and sorghum and some commodities for trading. Her problem of marketing is lack of persons or assistants to take care of her children when she goes to market, although her mother helps her most of the times. The main problem she encounters in the trading of honey and tobacco is the increasing purchasing prices of both commodities at Shewarobit, making it difficult to get market profitably from her poor customers in Kumame, Gefram and Beadu kebeles.*

4.4 Constraints to off-/non-farm income

According to the findings of this research, the major constraints to off-farm activities are shown in Table 8. The two major constraints to off/non-farm activities in SRG are lack of acceptance because of tradition and culture (27.5%), which does not appreciate non/off-farm activities, and lack of skill and entrepreneurship (22.5%). Similarly, the two major constraints of off-farm activities in Dulecha are lack of capital/credit (32.5%) and lack of employment (22.5%).

Table 8: Major constraints to off-/non-farm income activities

Constraint	SRG	Dulecha
Lack of employment	8 (20.0%)	9 (22.5%)
Lack of capital/credit	5 (12.5%)	13 (32.5%)
Lack of market for non-farm products	-	2 (5.0%)
Lack of skill and entrepreneurship	9 (22.5%)	6 (15%)
Discouragement by local culture	11 (27.5%)	-
Full time engagement in on-farm, thus lack of labor for non/off-farm work	1 (2.5%)	5 (12.5%)
Poor physical accessibility of markets due to lack of means of transportation	2 (5.0%)	1 (2.5%)
Lack of tradition in off-farm/non-farm activities	4 (10.0%)	1 (2.5%)
Not sure	-	4 (10.0%)

SOURCE: Own survey, August 2010

5 Market Interactions between Pastoral Lowland and Highland Economic Systems

5.1 Markets and market linkages of pastoralists and highland farmers

Both lowland pastoralists and highland farmers produce goods and services which they exchange to each other depending on their needs and demand. The major goods produced by pastoralists are mainly livestock and livestock products, while those goods produced and supplied by highland farmers are mainly grains and horticultural products. Towns located in highland and/or in lowland-highland interface areas do supply goods and services such as food, clothing, household commodities (furniture, utensils, ropes, etc.) farm tools, drugs and medicines, repair and maintenance services.

The main animal marketplace for pastoralists of SRG *woreda* is Shewarobit, whose access is limited due to the recurrent ethnic conflict that prevailed in the area. In the past two years, however, there is tranquility due to the deployment of police and militia. The construction of marketplace in Kumame town/center of

SRG *woreda*, which was undergoing during the survey year (2010) with assistance of FarmAfrica is considered to be a useful measure to create alternative marketplace and to minimize conflicts faced in route to Shewarobit. It is also indicated by the key informants that establishing marketplace at Kumame could help to minimize conflicts. Highlanders and traders who come to Kumame may not be threatened by Afar people, as Afar culture respect guests who come to their place for trading and marketing purposes. This opinion is also shared by a long time expert of FarmAfrica at Kumame, who also observed that when conditions are relatively peaceful highland traders visit markets in pastoral areas. If marketplaces are made convenient with all required services such as water trough for animals, shades for the people, grain marketing quarter, roads and means of transportation, inspection and strong policing of marketing practices and the marketplace, two way movements to marketplaces (Shewarobit and Kumame) would promote pastoral production and peaceful market interactions. The following narration is the continuation of that of Ato Hamedo of SRG *woreda* in relation to his marketing practices.

Ato Hamedo sells his goats at Shewarobit market, which he visits twice a month on average. This is a loose estimate of the respondent probably showing his inclination or desire. He spends two days before reaching Zuti livestock marketplace in Shewarobit town. He goes in group through Afar land spending a night on the road, mostly at Ade-Ele Hingig, an Afar *kebele*, bordering Shewarobit. He goes for marketing particularly when his family faces shortage of food, requiring money to buy some food. Traders who come from different places including as far places as Debre Berhan are the ones who buy his goats. From Shewarobit market he buys grains such as wheat, sorghum and maize. Fear or suspicion of attack from Amhara individuals on the road is a key threat that makes marketing at Shewarobit risky and uncertain. He mentioned that an Afar travels to Shewarobit market is threatened about his safety. The long distance that he or his family members travels to reach Shewarobit is also a serious problem that takes much time and energy. The long distance trekking of animals to marketplace often causes animals to emaciate and lose health. Other problems at the marketplace he indicated include lack of water for animals and people, lack of food canteens, lack of shade to protect people from sun heat, absence of transportation vehicles for animals. He mentioned, however, that space of the livestock marketplace (Zuti) is sufficient and that there is good policing service to keep law and order at the marketplace.

The highlanders from far places like Debresina, Moja-na-Wadera, Basonworana, Jiru (Enewary) and Jihur, Merhabete, Moferwuha and Jamma do come to Shewarobit, mostly in June, to buy cattle from pastoral areas. Shewarobit is a hub for livestock trade and a livestock dispatching center to different destinations such as Sudan through Antsokia, Mekele, and Somalia. A very crucial problem with livestock trading is animal diseases that spread, since there is no quarantine service at Shewarobit. Competition for controlling and managing quarantine service among various centers (e.g. Shewarobit Municipality and Kewot *woreda* administration) has delayed the establishment of quarantine center and delivery of the service. This situation seems to aggravate the inefficiency of livestock marketing and trading in the area.

An observation in the markets indicated that the animal marketplace (Zuti) in Shewarobit town is less organized and lacks proper infrastructure and services, such as shades as protection from sun heat, water trough for animals and proper organization of compartments of the marketplace for various types of animals. The major problem emerging regarding Zuti marketplace, as indicated by the key informant, is lack of clarity as to whether it is the *woreda* or the town municipality that should own and manage the marketplace; and this is compounded by the fact that the town is given a municipality status. The competition for control of the marketplace is because of the financial income (tax and related incomes) to be accrued from the market services. Some examples of the situation in this regard can help to understand challenges better.

Abayaatir is a market place in Rasa area bordering SRG *woreda*. The market is visited by pastoralists, farmers, traders and consumers from lowland and highland areas. Abayaatir marketplace has no shade that protects market participants from sun heat. There is, however, a pond around the market place that serves as a good water source for the animals in the market.

Ankober farmers do visit Aliyuamba, a market center in Ankobr *woreda*, but they do not visit Gachine, town of Argoba-Liyu *Woreda*, and Dulecha markets. Dulecha pastoralists do visit Aliyuamba market and Gachinie, but not Ankober market. Aliyuamba is a market town, interfacing Ankober highland and Argoba /Gachinie lowland and Dulecha Afar lowlands. Both Ankober and Dulecha pastoralists and agro-pastoralists can exchange any products they need at Aliyuamba market center. Moreover, long distance and risk of conflict could probably be some of the reasons for Dulecha pastoralists not to go to Ankober center and for Ankober farmers not to visit Dulecha market.

Argoba communities in Argoba Liyu *woreda* are predominantly settled agro-pastoralists and do sell their animals at Tachmetekliya market known by the name of Abule, Gachine, and Haramba and Gorgo town markets located in Ankober *woreda*. They buy their goods, including food grains, mainly from Haramba, Gorgo, Aliyuamba and Gachine market centers.

A key informant from Ankober Agriculture and Rural Development Office indicated his observation with regard to market linkages. According to him, Dulecha pastoralists visit markets located at Gorgo, Aliyuamba and Haramba, all within Ankober *woreda*, to sell cattle and buy wheat and maize. Pastoralists sell male calves to lowland Ankober farmers. Ankober traders go to Aliyuamba market to buy beef cattle brought by Afar pastoralists for sale after fattening the cattle. Pastoralists in Dulecha do also go to Awash Sebat market to sell animals, mainly goats and camel, and purchase some other consumer commodities. The major marketing problem for Dulecha pastoralists is lack of proper roads that connect market centers and pastoralists and lack of means of transportation. The following discussion with a highland farmer illustrates the market relations highland farmers have with neighboring lowland pastoralists and markets.

> *Ato Yemane Minda of Ankober Woreda, aged 25 with six grade of education and family size of three, is engaged in farming and a small business of his own. He produces twice a year in Meher and Belg seasons. The commodities he produces include faba bean, barley, field pea, lentil linseed, wheat, potato, red beet, carrot and cabbages. His family produces and sells eggs and honey and collects and sells firewood. He sells his products at various markets depending on his convenience, volume and type of products and price. He sells barley and faba bean at Debre Berhan market. At his kebele market (Boled), he sells eggs and chicken. He goes also to Ankober market, and sometimes to Aliyuamba to buy teff and goat and sell barley. He indicated the major constraints to marketing to be lack of transport and expensive price of transport fares to go to markets located in areas far from Ankober.*

5.2 Commodities exchanged between pastoral and highland communities

Crop marketing

According to the findings from the household survey, the dominant marketplaces where SRG agro-pastoralists sell any crop products are Shewrobit and Abayatir, as reported by 17.5% and 15.0% respondents, respectively. The remaining pastoralists did not mention any particular market they visited. Similarly, 7.5% and 10% of sample respondents in Dulecha *woreda* market crops in Aliyuamba and Gachinie, respectively. The remaining did not participate in crop marketing. As expected crop production and marketing is not a major livelihood source. The agro-pastoralists are the ones who sell crop grains whenever they need some cash, although the production is not even adequate for home consumption.

Marketed beef animals

As indicated by 82.5% and 10% of sample pastoralists in SRG *woreda*, the major beef animals sold between 2008-10 were goats and camels respectively. Goats and beef cattle are also the two important animals sold during the period as they constitute 85% and 10% of the responses of the sample Dulecha households respectively.

Shoats: 65% and 27.5% of SRG pastoralists sell their shoats at Shewarobit and Abayaatir markets respecively. Similarly, 67.5% of the pastoralists in Dulecha sell shoats at Dulecha town market, while 32.5% of them mentioned Gachini as a major market place for shoats.

Cattle: As reported by 80% of sample households, Shewarobit is the major cattle market for SRG pastoralists, while 72.5% of and 22.5% Dulecha pastoralists sell cattle at Dulecha and Aliyuamba markets respectively. Thus, Dulecha is an important cattle market place for Dulecha pastoralists. Dulecha pastoralists seem to have considerable market linkage with Aliyuamba in Ankober *woreda*.

Camel: The first important marketplace where SRG pastoralists sell camel is Shewarobit market, as reported by 80% of pastoralist respondents. Ten percent of them indicated that they sell at Dulecha town market. Similarly, 65% of Dulecha pastoralists sell camel at Dulecha town market, the remaining did not mention any market for the sale of camel. Dulecha seems to be an important camel market for both SRG and Dulecha pastoralists.

Animal products marketed

Pastoralists were asked to indicate the first important animal product they sold in the last three years before the survey time. Accordingly, 20% and 10% of the Dulecha sample respondents indicated that they were involved in selling goat milk and eggs respectively. The large majority (95%) of the respondents in SRG indicated that they did not participate in selling animal products during the three years before the survey time; only 5% of them indicated to have sold eggs and cow milk.

Milk: Cow milk is not as such marketed. Only one pastoralist in SRG and two in Dulecha *woreda* reported that they sold their cow milk to their respective *woreda* towns, Kumame and Dulecha, respectively. Twenty percent of Dulecha sample respondents reported that they sold goat milk in Dulecha town. No pastoralist in SRG reported any sale of goat milk.

Figure 4: Livestock market in Shewrobit town (Zuti)

While livestock in general are the major source of income, camel and animal products, such as milk and eggs, are not a significant source of cash income. In other words, shoats and cattle are the major marketable produces that link pastoralists with the highland economy. Milk production and marketing seem to require more development intervention and effort. Shoats and cattle production and marketing is also an important economic sector that deserves increased attention in terms of its productivity and market infrastructure development.

The long distance to livestock market places and lack of means of transportation are the two factors that limit livestock production and marketing, and hence their poor linkage with the highland economic system. For example, pastoralists in SRG require 2-3 days to travel to the Shewarobit livestock market, while Dulecha pastoralists spend 6 – 9 hours to reach Aliyuamba market in Ankober *woreda*. Moreover, all the respondents in both *woredas* reported that they traveled to town markets within their *woredas* by foot, except one pastoralist among the Dulecha sample who reported that he used pack animals as means of transportation. Animal transportation by truck is totally absent in the areas, even to truck animals to distant animal market places like Shewarobit.

5.3   Pastoral marketing problems

Inaccessibility is the major marketing problem that constrains pastoralists'
interaction with the highland economic system. Poor physical accessibility of
markets (55%) and lack of transport (30%) were reported as key problems of the
sample pastoralists in SRG. High price of crop commodities and shortage of
money are the other market related problems mentioned by some respondents.
Similarly, 36.8%, 31.8% and 28.9% of the Dulecha sample pastoralists indicated
that shortage of money, poor physical accessibility of markets and lack of means
of transportation respectively are the problems they face in buying food crops.

Livestock marketing by pastoralists also encounters multiple problems. As
reported by respondents of SRG *woreda*, remoteness of livestock marketplaces
(75%) and insufficient livestock production (17.5%) are the primary constraints
of livestock marketing. For Dulecha pastoralists, lack of market, low price of
livestock, remoteness of markets and insufficiency of livestock production are
the primary problems of livestock marketing as indicated by 45%, 20%, 15%
and 15% of the sample pastoralists respectively.

Problems of animal product marketing

Cow milk: The most important problems encountered in cow milk marketing
within the pastoral economic system and with the highland economic system, as
reported by 27.5% 17.5%, 15% and 15% of the respondents in SRG are
respectively cultural unacceptability of milk selling, lack of tradition
(uncommon) of milk selling, lack of market and remoteness of markets located
in the highland economic system. For Dulecha pastoralists, the major problem of
marketing cow milk is low milk production for the market (77.5%).

Camel milk: The major constraint of camel milk marketing within pastoral and
highland economic systems, as indicated by the large proportion (95%) of SRG
sample respondents, is cultural unacceptability of selling milk. Similarly, 70% of
Dulecha sample pastoralists indicated the same factor as the major constraint of
camel milk marketing. However, 17.5% of the sample households in Dulecha
indicated that they do not know the reason for the problem, while 5% of them
attributed the reason to lack of tradition of milk selling in the area.

In both *woredas*, inaccessibility of livestock markets, lack of transport and
insufficient livestock production are identified as important constraints to
livestock marketing. Lack of cash income and far distance of market places are
mentioned by the sample pastoralists as problems that constrain purchasing of
food and non-food consumables from highland economic systems. An important
implication and observation in this regard is that opening and enabling easy

market access would be instrumental to motivate pastoralists to enhance their livestock production and engage in other income generating activities.

On the other hand, production of livestock and livestock products is highly constrained by multiple factors. As indicated by the response of the respondents in SRG sample population, the major constraints of cow milk production are low milk yielding cows (35%), lack of feeds or grazing land (27.5%) and lack adequate number of milk cows (17.5%). Similarly, 50.0% and 42.5% of the respondents in Dulecha *woreda* indicated that lack of high milk yielding cows and shortage of feeds and grazing land, respectively, are the most important limiting factors for cow milk production.

For camel milk production, the major constraints are shortage of feeds and grazing land and lack of camels, as reported by 55% and 27.5% of the respondents in Dulecha *woreda* respectively. Similarly, 35%, 27.5% and 12% of the respondents in SRG *woreda* indicated that lack of high yielding camels, shortage of feeds and grazing land and lack of water, respectively, are the major problems that constrain camel milk production (Table 9).

Table 9: Major constraints of cow milk and camel milk production in the study sites

Constraint	SRG *Woreda*	Dulecha *Woreda*
Cow milk production		
Poor milk yielding cows	14 (35.0%)	20 (50.0%)
Shortage of feeds/grazing land	11 (27.5 %)	17 (42.5%)
Water shortage	5 (12.5%)	-
Diseases	3 (7.55)	1 (2.5%)
Shortage of cows	7 (17.5%)	2 (5%)
Camel milk production		
Poor milk yielding camels	14 (35.0%)	4 (10.0%)
Shortage of feeds/grazing land	11 (27.5 %)	22 (55%)
Water shortage	5 (12.5%)	-
Diseases	4 (10%)	-
Shortage of camels	6 (15%)	11(27.5%)
I don't know	-	3 (7.5%)

SOURCE: Own survey, August 2010

5.4   Highland farmer products purchased by lowland pastoralists

Pastoralists and agro-pastoralist do buy essential products produced by highland
producers. These products include mainly food grains and some highland
vegetables like onion and shallot. These products are found often in markets
located in the highland-lowland interface town markets, such as Shewarobit in
Kewat *woreda* and Aliyuamba in Ankober *woreda*. All the sample households in
SRG and 37.5% of respondents of Dulecha *woreda* indicated that the major
highland crops they purchase are food grains, such as *teff* and sorghum. The
second important highland crops purchased by lowland pastoralists as mentioned
by eight (20%) SRG respondents and four (10%) Dulecha sample respondents
are vegetables, including onions and pulses, respectively.

The major markets visited by pastoralists of SRG *woreda* to buy products are
Shewarobit and Abayaatir located in the lowland-highland interface area in
Kewot *woreda*. From Shewrobit and Abayaatir markets, pastoralists buy also
non-staple food items such as oil, sugar, salt, detergents, clothes and other
consumables.

The SRG and Dulecha sample respondents also mentioned that they buy inputs
such as farm tools (hoe, sickles, plough beam, etc.), seeds, fertilizer and
pesticides from Shewrobit and Aliyuamba markets respectively.

The sample respondents were asked about their assessment about the magnitude
of products they buy from highland markets. As shown in Table 10, 52.5% and
45% of the respondents respectively in SRG *woreda* indicated that the quantity
of products they buy were of high and medium level. And only 10% and 27.5%
of the respondents in Dulecha *woreda* pointed out that the magnitude was of
high and medium level, respectively. In Dulecha *woreda*, 55 % of the
respondents indicated that they did not buy any products from highland markets.

Table 10: The magnitude of products bought in highland markets as assessed by
sample pastoralists

Magnitude	SRG	Dulecha
High	21 (52.5%)	4 (10%)
Medium	18 (45%)	11 (27.5%)
Low	1(2.5%)	3 (7.5%)
None	-	22 (55%)

SOURCE: Own survey, August 2010

Similarly, the pastoralists were asked to compare the quantity of products they sell in highland and lowland markets. Accordingly, while 82.5% of the SRG *woreda* sample respondents indicated that they sold higher quantities of products in highland markets than what they sell in lowland markets, only 10% of the Dulecha sample pastoralists mentioned that they sold higher amounts of products in highland markets compared to that they sold in low land market places. In the case of Dulecha, most respondents (60%) indicated that they did not sell products in highland markets at all.

Thus, generally SRG pastoralists have relatively stronger linkages with highland markets in terms of both selling and buying products compared to Dulecha pastoralists. Dulecha's poor linkage could partly be attributed to the isolation of the communities/*woreda* due to road and transportation problems, and probably partly to the availability of alternative markets in Awash areas.

5.5   Services accessed by pastoralists in highland markets or towns

Most of the institutions and business organizations that provide services such as education, health, tool repair, hair dressing, etc. are located in highland towns or market centers. The pastoralists, therefore, were asked to point out the magnitude of service they access in highland markets/towns. The data analysis showed that only 10% and 15% of the respondents in SRG and Dulecha *woreda*, respectively, got farm tool repair service entirely from highland marketplace, and a significant proportion (67.5%) of the respondents in both *woredas* did not get the service from the highland towns at all. Similarly, 95% of the respondents in Dulecha *woreda* indicated that they did not go to highland towns for hair dressing, while 50% of the SRG respondents indicated that they accessed the service in highland towns.

School and health service needs of pastoralists are to some extent obtained from highland towns. The findings of the analysis showed that only 15% of pastoralists in SRG rely entirely on the towns in the highland for their health service requirement, while 37.5% and 40 % of the respondents, respectively, indicated that they got half and quarter of the total services they need from towns in the highland. Similarly, 17.5% and 15% of Dulecha respondents indicated, respectively, that they got about half and quarter of their health service requirement from highland towns. Close to half of the respondents (47.5%) in Dulecha *woreda* did not go to highland centers for health service at all. With regard to access to schooling service for pastoral children, 57.5% and 27.5% of the SRG respondents respectively indicated that they got about half and quarter of the schooling service in highland centers. In the case of Dulecha pastoralists, 87.5% of them reported that their children did not go to highland centers for schooling.

The sample pastoralists were also asked to indicate the whereabouts of high school (9-12 grade) education and hospital-level health care services they get from. As shown in Table 11, SRG sample pastoralists get high school for their children (95%) and hospital service (100%) mainly from neighboring non-Afar zones and *woredas*. On the other hand, Dulecha pastoralists got high school service from within their zone as reported by 85% of sample respondents; and 30% of them indicated that they got hospital service from within their zone, the rest getting from neighboring non-Afar zones and *woredas*.

Table 11: Location of high school and health services accessed by pastoralists

Source/whereabout	High school place		Hospital level health service	
	SRG	Dulecha	SRG	Dulecha
From within Afar zone/*woreda*	1 (2.5%)	34 (85%)	-	12 (30%)
Other zone/*woreda* in Afar	1 (2.5%)	6 (15%)	-	-
Neighboring non-Afar/ highland zone/*woreda*	38 (95%)	-	40 (100%)	28 (70%)

SOURCE: Own survey, August 2010

With regard to extension service, pastoralists in SRG indicated that they did not receive any support during the year before the survey time. The four sample pastoralists in Dulecha who indicated that they had received extension services during the year, did get the service within their own *woreda*. It seems that the pastoralists in both *woredas* were not getting adequate extension services; and this could be a serious constraint to pastoral development.

Veterinary and drug supply services are important inputs for livestock production. Pastoralists access such inputs either from their locality or from other towns or *woreda* centers. The survey data revealed that all respondents in Dulecha did not go to highland towns or centers for veterinary services. On the other hand, 10% of the respondents in SRG *woreda* got half of their veterinary service, while another 10% of the respondents got a quarter of the service they required from highland towns or centers. Moreover, 67.5% of the respondents in the SRG *woreda* indicated that they did not go to highland centers for veterinary service. With regard to access to livestock drugs, 97.5% of the sample respondents in Dulecha *woreda* indicated that they did not go to highland centers or towns for drugs at all. In the case of SRG *woreda*, 42.5% and 20% of the sample respondents respectively pointed out that they got or purchased half and a quarter of livestock drugs from highland towns or markets. Thus, compared to SRG pastoralists, pastoralists in Dulecha were less reliant on highland markets for livestock drugs.

The study also assessed major shopping places for food items and drinks consumed by households. As the data analysis indicated, while a large proportion (77.5%) of Dulecha sample pastoralists did not go to highland towns for food and drinks, 87.5% of the respondents in SRG mentioned to have visited highland centers for shopping food and drinks. Ten percent of Dulecha respondents indicated they visited highland towns to buy a quarter of their total consumption of food and drinks.

Pastoralists do also buy non-food consumption goods from shops found within their vicinities or visit shops outside their area in the highland markets when they go for marketing. SRG sample pastoralists seem to visit highland market towns for shopping more frequently compared to Dulecha pastoralists. As the data analysis showed, 37.5% and 42.5% of the SRG sample pastoralists did shop at highland towns or centers all and half of the commodities they required, respectively. On the other hand, 62.5% of Dulecha sample pastoralists did not go to highland market towns or centers for shopping at all, while 30% of them indicated that they went to highland areas to buy half of the non-food commodities they required.

The existing formal linkages and collaboration forged by lowland pastoral Dulecha *woreda* and highland Ankober *woreda* exemplify the efforts made to strengthen institutional linkages between lowland and highland systems. Key development sectors of Ankober, such as agriculture, health, finance, justice, etc extend support in the respective sectors in terms of training, facilitating transfer of technology and inputs (e.g. seedlings) to lowland areas. Similar services are also rendered by Kewot *woreda* institutions to SRG *woreda*. Such institutional linkages would have contributions in the effort of mitigating conflicts between pastoral and highland communities, facilitating economic interactions.

As indicated by a key informant from Ankober *woreda* agricultural and rural development office, the Ankober *woreda* finance, agriculture, justice and other offices do support their counterparts in Dulecha *woreda*. These supportive links include controlling crop insects like locust breakout, distribution of tree and fodder tree seedlings, distribution of drugs and expert service at times when animal diseases breakout (e.g. goat disease). In addition, peace committees of both *woredas* meet and exchange experiences and design joint work programs.

The finance office of Ankober *woreda* supports its Dulecha counter part in
financial planning and control. Besides, Afar pastoralists have recently started
producing charcoal from a weed tree called Prosopis *Juliflora* (locally known as
Woyane) for sale to highlanders. These and other types of links would also help
to improve relationships between Afar pastoralists and the highland farmers and
also contribute to controlling and reducing conflict incidences.

5.6   Constraints to economic and market interactions between lowland and highland economies

This section discusses factors and conditions that hinder pastoral and highland
economic interactions on the basis of the responses and perceptions of the
sample respondents in the study *woredas* (Table 12) supplemented with views of
key informants. As reported by 57.5% and 50% sample respondents of SRG and
Dulecha *woreda* respectively, distance of highland markets is the major problem
that limits economic and market interactions of the two economic systems. This
is followed by conflict problems in SRG and lack of means of transportation in
Dulecha *woreda*. The findings imply the need for more attention to resolve
problems of remote market places, addressing conflicts and lack of means of
transportation.

Table 12: Major constraints to market and economic interactions between
lowland and highland economic systems

Constraint	SRG	Dulecha
Far distance of highland markets/towns	23 (57.5%)	20 (50%)
Conflicts existing between the two communities	10 (25%)	7 (17.5%)
Lack of products to exchange with	-	3 (7.5%)
Lack of means of transportation	7 (17.5%)	10 (25%)

SOURCE: Own survey, August 2010

Regarding constraints, the discussion made with an input expert from Ankober
woreda Agriculture and Rural Development Office indicated that the major
constraints include increase in the price of inputs, the financial difficulty young
farmers experience in accessing the inputs; unavailability of agricultural inputs
nearby at fair prices; and inconvenient topography for irrigation infrastructure
development despite the fact that there are many rivers (e.g. Ayrara) and streams
in the highland Ankober area. In addition, interventions by middlemen in

distorting prices and providing misleading market information were also singled out as constraints. In particular, middlemen are blamed for adulterating commodities to maximize profit and moving products in an illegal manner with the intention of evading taxes and grabbing advantages over licensed and tax paying traders. These issues revealed the interwoven institutional and physical constraints that work against attempts to increase production of small highland farmers to be supplied to the market. By way of solution, improving and building institutional capacity to supply inputs and market information and promoting investment in irrigation infrastructure need to be considered as part of future efforts in agricultural development in the highland Ankober area. This can enhance market and economic linkages of the highland and pastoral economic systems.

Discussions with the PADET officer in Ankober *woreda* brought out different types of constraints that limit market linkages between pastoral Dulecha and highland Ankober *woredas*. The discussant identified conflict as a key problem. As shown in Table 12, however, a lower proportion of pastoral household survey respondents mentioned conflict as an important problem hampering market linkages compared with the percentage of respondents who indicated access and distance to highland market as a key constraint to an effective linkage between pastoral and highland systems. In summary, according to the officer, the major constraints that hinder market participation are conflicts, lack of road infrastructure, weak local markets (poor purchasing power of buyers), no or limited number of private investors, vulnerability of the pastoralist community to drought, and cultural stereotypes towards business relationships.

5.6.1   Conflict-related constraints and dynamics

Survey households were asked whether they encountered conflicts when they moved to remote places in search of grazing land and water. 75% of the sampled pastoralists in SRG indicated that they faced conflicts, while only 5% indicated that they did not encounter any conflict. In SRG, 20% of the respondents indicated that they had not moved to other places during the three years previous to the survey time. Similarly, as given in Table 13, 32.5% of the sample respondents in Dulecha *woreda* indicated that they faced conflicts during the last three years before the survey time. Also, 57.5% of the Dulecha sample pastoralists did not move to distant places to look for pasture and water during the three years before the survey time. Out of the 30 SRG pastoralists who experienced conflicts, 10, 13 and 7 of them faced conflicts in 2007/08, 2008/09 and 2008/09 respectively. Out of the 13 Dulecha pastoralists who were trapped in conflicts, 7 faced conflicts in 2007/08, while there was only one such incident in 2008/09.

Table 13: Responses as to whether pastoralists encountered conflicts while moving to a remote area in search of pasture and water during the past three years

Description	SRG	Dulecha
Not encountered	2 (5%)	4 (10%)
Encountered	30 (75%)	13 (32.5%)
Did not move to remote place	8 (20%)	23 (57.5%)

SOURCE: Own survey, August 2010

With regard to causes of conflict, 60% of the pastoralists in SRG and 61.5% of Dulecha pastoralists who faced conflicts indicated that the main reason was reluctance of the hosting community to allow the livestock of migrant pastoralists to graze in what they consider their territory. The other reason indicated by 33.5% and 38.5% the respondents in SRG and Dulecha *woreda* respectively was competition for limited grazing pasture and water. This result implies that access to the key resources - grazing land/feeds and water - is one of the crucial factors in mitigating conflicts between pastoralists and highland farming communities.

Trends of conflicts

The dynamics of the conflict situation in the study *woredas* was discussed with various key informants. It was known that relation between Afar and the neighboring Amhara farmers in Kewot *woreda* was volatile and conflict is recurrent. In the past, there had been peace agreements for relatively long periods but this was breached two weeks before the survey date. The main cause for the resurgence of conflict was the killing of an Afar herder by an Amhara farmer. According to one pastoralist named Hamedo, pasture and water are not the major causes of conflict as such. The basic underlying cause seems to be the culture and tradition of taking revenge against those who perpetrate killings against the other side. Under such tradition and culture, a member of a family whose relative or family member was killed, irrespective of when it might have happened, is always poised to revenge by killing somebody related to the family or to the clan of the assumed killer. An Afar who kills an Amhara and vice-versa is considered to be a hero by the community/clan and is considered as a popular and epitomized personality. For an Afar pastoralist, killing an 'enemy' of a family or clan has been considered a sign of heroism and patriotism, and that particular individual is proud to show it off by different decorative items, such as rings and other symbols on sword-like defense weapon (known as *Gille*) to reveal his epitomized personality to his clan community.

According to the perception of a highland farmer from Wofkelle *kebele*, Kewot *woreda*, pastoralists have a claim that most lowlands from Rasa area up to Yelen *kebele* belonged to them about 100 years ago. In turn, highlanders claim that the areas were unoccupied and inhabited by big game animals including lions before their forefathers developed the area for settlement and farming. The informant further indicated that strengthening market linkages through construction of roads, availing means of transport and good *kebele* governance and administration would contribute to broadening market linkages between farmers and pastoralists and minimize conflicts.

Similarly, discussions with key informants in Ankober and Aliyuamba revealed a similar opinion to that gathered in Kewot and Semurobi-Gelealo *woredas*. The discussion pointed out the need for facilitating pastoralists and the youth participation in diverse economic activities which would motivate them to engage in building their assets and wealth, and to disassociate from practice of revenging and other socially harmful and undesirable engagements. In an in-depth interview, another farmer in Ankober by the name Yemane discussed the historical and traditional conflicts between the Amhara and Afar. According to his observation and perception, the Amharas are not interested in killing any Afar out of the need for revenging incidents in the past but they rather want to link with them in business. In his opinion, there should be peaceful and reconciliation-based relations, and suggested that government should be responsible for controlling such problems and providing strong and implementable legal justice.

A discussion with an officer of PADET-ActionAid brought out the efforts being done by the non-state actors in mitigating livelihood problems of communities in the highland Ankober and lowland Dulecha areas. He indicated that in conjunction with promotion of hygienic water supply and hygienic circumcision practices, the non-state actors (NSA) were actively working to raise the level of awareness of pastoralists in Dulecha on harmful practices, such as female genital mutilation (FGM) and songs that belittle and provoke other groups during the occasion of circumcision. According to this informant, songs that applaud vindictive killings and instigate others to seek revenge for their relatives' blood who were killed decades before by unknown Amhara individuals must be discouraged. There are also training programs that emphasize the negative effects of such songs because they deter people from productive and economic engagements and constructive social relations. He has observed that such singing practices are now declining, and that the Afar community is gradually accepting the undesirability of such songs.

Effects of conflicts

The negative effects of conflicts were also indicated by the sample households
heads. Accordingly, in SRG, 48.2% of the respondents indicated that the major
effects of the social conflict are the plundering of livestock, and (37.5%) killing
of people. In Dulecha, the harm inflicted by conflicts was killing of people and
livestock plunder as reported by 42.1% and 26.3% of sample respondents
respectively (Table 14).

Table 14: Effects of conflicts between lowland pastoralists and highland farmers

Harm inflicted	SRG	Dulecha
Livestock plunder	27 (47.2 %)	5 (26.3%)
Livestock killing	2 (3.6%)	1 (5.3%)
Penalty payment	-	2 (10.5%)
Weapon robbery	3 (5.4%)	-
Killing people	21 (37.5%)	8 (42.1%)
Wounding persons	2 (3.6%)	-
None	1 (1.8%)	

SOURCE: Own survey, August 2010

5.6.2   Institutions involved in conflict management

Important issues that were addressed in connection with conflicts and the
resulting damage have been the mechanisms and institutions employed to
resolve conflicts and mitigating the ensuing harm to communities and
individuals. According to the findings, 34.5% and 20.7% of the respondents in
SRG identified administrative systems and traditional means respectively as
major mechanisms employed to resolve conflicts that occur during seasonal
migration and the resulting harms. In Dulecha, the dominant mechanisms used
are traditional means and administrative system as reported by 70% and 20% of
the sample respondents respectively. In the case of SRG, a third of the
respondents (37.9%) indicated that migrants who venture in search of pasture
and water would often return to the same area without settling earlier conflicts
(Table 15).

Table 15: The major mechanisms of resolving conflicts during migration to pasture land

Mechanism	SRG	Dulecha
Traditional way	6 (20.7%)	7 (70%)
Formal judicial court process	2 (6.9%)	-
Administrative process	10 (34.5%)	2 (20%)
Agreement between the conflicting groups	-	1 (10%)
Returning back without settling conflicts	11 (37.9%)	-

SOURCE: Own survey, August 2010

Pastoralists in SRG seem more exposed to conflicts and harms compared to pastoralists in Dulecha. On the other hand, Dulecha pastoralists seem to employ more of traditional means of resolving conflicts, compared to SRG pastoralists. The pattern seems to be associated with the level of interactions between lowland pastoralists and the highland economic system; and this can be partially explained by the fact that Dulecha *woreda* is poorly connected with its neighboring highland system relative to SRG pastoralists.

The sample survey respondents also identified some of the institutions involved in resolving conflicts. As shown in Table 15, the major institutions involved in resolving conflicts in SRG are government administration followed by elders' councils and clan leaders as indicated by 77.5%, 12.5% and 10 % of the sample respondents respectively. In Dulecha, 72.5% and 27.5% of the sample respondents indicated that elders' councils and government administration respectively are the major institutions involved in conflict resolution. Some respondents in SRG also mentioned that local and traditional religious institutions like Qalu or Qalicha are involved in conflict resolution. The full details are provided in Table 16.

Table 16: The major institutions involved in conflict resolution during migration
to pasture land

Institution	SRG	Dulecha
Elders council	5 (12.5%)	29 (72.5%)
Clan leaders	4 (10%)	-
Government administration	31 (77.5%)	11 (27.5%)

SOURCE: Own survey, August 2010

The respondents were also asked to indicate their first-choice conflict resolution mechanism. In SRG, 33 respondents (82.5 %) indicated that they preferred government administrative mechanisms, while 7 of them (17.5%) preferred traditional mechanisms. In the case of Dulecha, 22 (55.5%) and 15 (37.5%) of the respondents preferred traditional institutions and government administrative mechanisms respectively.

Pastoralists do have different reasons for preferring traditional institutions, government administrative mechanisms or judiciary (court) procedures in resolving conflicts. The reason given by half of (50%) of the respondents in SRG who chose traditional institutions is that they are much more efficient in resolving the problem peacefully. The other important reason as reported by 20% of SRG pastoralists is that elders' councils command a high degree of respect and acceptance among the community. In Dulecha, the main reason given by 31.3% of the respondents for preferring traditional ways of resolving conflicts has been the fact that the community has very strong ties with traditional institutions and relationships. In addition, the second highest proportion (21.9%) of respondents in Dulecha stated that elders' councils commanded a high degree of respect and acceptance.

Similarly, respondents have indicated their reason for choosing government administrative mechanisms for resolving conflicts. In SRG, the reason given by the highest proportion of respondents (42.3%) was the belief that government has authority and can systematically investigate the causes and deal with the perpetrators of conflicts. It can also take appropriate solutions and legal measures. The second highest proportion of respondents (26.9%) in the same *woreda* indicated that the government can solve the problem fast and without much delay.

In Dulecha *woreda*, the highest proportion of the sample respondents (50%) attributed the reason for preferring government administrative mechanism to their belief that government can solve the problem as immediately as the conflicts occur. The second highest proportion (35%) of the respondents attributed the reason for their choice of government mechanisms to stronger power that government has to take measures and control conflicts efficiently.

Information on existing formal and informal (customary) institutional interventions and practices employed in resolving conflicts were also gathered from key informants in each study *woreda*. As indicated by key informants, Peace Committees have been formed and involved at *woreda* and *kebele* levels in conflict resolution in Amhara and Afar regions for more than 15 years. The slight decline in conflicts observed by various key informants has been partly due to the efforts of the committees in raising the awareness of the communities about the harmful effects of conflicts.

Some NGOs like FarmAfrica in Semurobi-Gelealo *woreda* and PADET-ActionAid in Ankober *woreda* have programs to support peace building activities of peace committees formed by bordering regions and *woredas* in Amhara, Afar and Oromia. The organizations have sponsored annual meetings of peace committees and assisted the construction of office building to house these committees at Aliyuamba.

On the other hand, however, the key informants assessed the local public agencies like *woreda* Pastoral, Agricultural and Rural Development Offices and programs to be less useful in terms of offering relevant and appropriate services suitable for pastoral systems. The key informants also suggested that unless large scale investments in skilled manpower development and adaptive and dynamic development service programs (e.g. mobile veterinary systems) are designed and implemented effectively and efficiently, transformation of the pastoral system into commercial and productive enterprise would be less feasible. Having commercially interactive economic systems would have important contribution in easing the peace building efforts of conflict management institutions.

Offices of Conflict Prevention and Resolution under the *Woreda* Administration and Security Affairs were established in 2009 by governments of neighboring Amhara and Afar *woredas* (Kewot-SRG and Ankober-Argoba Liyu *woreda* and Dulecha of Afar *woreda*). The aim is to prevent conflicts and build peace and promote harmonious relationship between neighboring Afar and Amhara *woredas*. It is also intended to facilitate sector development relations between the highland Amhara *woredas* and neighboring lowland pastoral *woredas*. The office is also engaged in identifying those who offend rights of community members, jointly with neighboring *woreda* from both sides of the border. It monitors and facilitates the reconciliation process and helps in returning raided animals to owner households or communities by following up proper judiciary procedures to penalize right offenders.

A good example of activities pertaining to promotion of economic relations and peace building is the work done by SRG and Kewot *woreda* Offices of Administration and Security Affairs. These offices have jointly divided the large tract of land named Dahoda located at the border *kebeles* of both *woredas* into two giving one part to the Afar community and the remaining half to Kureberet *kebele* of Kewot *woreda*. In the farming season, the Afar share of Dahoda land was cultivated by Amhara farmers through a sharecropping arrangement with the Afar community. Encouraged by the presence of a peace accord, Afar pastoralists visit Kureberet market located at nearby farmers *kebele* to sell small goats (*Girgire*) and locally made ropes. They in turn buy from the market dried *Injera* (thin pan like cake made out of *teff* or sorghum grain) and sugar. Despite these beneficial interactions, however, both groups do not trust each other.

The Conflict Prevention and Resolution Office monitors trends of conflicts and damages caused. As the records kept by the Administration and Security Affairs Office of Kewot *woreda* showed, there was a decline in cases of homicide and property damage or raid in the last three years (Appendix Tables 1 and 2). This is attributed to various efforts exerted by the communities through establishing peace committees and non-state actors (e.g. FarmAfrica) Development interventions For example, as observed at the time of the study survey, FarmAfrica supports promotion of marketing and market linkages by financing market place development in Kumame town of SRG *woreda*.

The Office of Conflict Prevention and Resolution of the Kewot *woreda* reported that there were five human fatalities incurred by Amhara communities - Sefiberet, Kureberet and Abayaatir - in 2009/10, while only one Afar individual was harmed during the same year. In the same year, transfers of alleged offenders to the respective regional justice bodies were also carried out. Accordingly, out of five suspected Amhara offenders, three were transferred, one was killed by police while resisting surrender and the other was arrested. On the Afar side, out of four suspected offenders, one was transferred to Kewot *woreda* police, and the three suspected offenders were not apprehended. Regarding fatalities in 2008/09, six Afar and three Amhara persons were killed due to acts of revenge.

Discussions held with three key informants and members, one of whom is an Afar, of the joint Peace Committee for the three *woredas* – Ankober, Argoba-Liyu and Dulecha – on the causes and nature of conflicts were revealing.

Although competition over water and pasture in highland areas was the immediate cause of conflict, there were also other equally very important reasons that go beyond the demand for pasture and water. According to the informants, the underlying causes of conflicts are the bad feeling the Afar retained from their forefathers/parents who were then penalized heavily by the feudal landlords/administrators when they refused to pay taxes and levies. Such measures in the last century have led the Afar to harbor sentiments of a kind of grudge/and revenge against the Amhara people. Such explanation, of course, need to be further re-examined on the basis of data and information from various sources. The other reason mentioned was the fact that the Afar culture demands the killing of a person before an Afar adult marries. A man who has not killed an Amhara or other non-Afar person was often considered to be inadequate to marry and is ridiculed. Another cultural practice that engenders conflicts is livestock raiding. An Afar who raids animals of non-Afars is often privileged for marriage. Thus, raiding animals belonging to 'others' has been a source of accumulating animal wealth and pride. Of course, this is an easy means of getting wealth, especially for those who are not hard working.

Suggestions on measures of resolving resource related conflicts

A number of sample respondents were asked to give their suggestions on measures that can alleviate resource-related conflicts in general. As shown in Table 17, the measures suggested by a considerable proportion of sample respondents in SRG are enabling the society to involve in off/non-farm activities (18.8%), improving government policy on use of grazing land and water (18.8%), maximizing operational efficiency of peace keeping committees, and making concerted efforts by government and community elders to resolve conflicts. In the case of Dulecha *woreda*, the suggestions in the order of proportion of respondents that mentioned each suggestion include making concerted efforts by government and community elders (28.6%), placing government law enforcement forces to take immediate action (23.8%), and strengthening the traditional participation of communities in resolving social problems (14.3%).

Table 17: Respondents' suggestions on alleviating resource-related conflicts

Suggestion	SRG	Dulecha
Government increase effective application of rules and regulations	1 (2.1%)	4 (9.5%)
Concerted efforts by government and community elders	7 (14.6%)	12 (28.6%)
Maximizing operational efficiency of peace keeping committee	8 (16.7%)	4(9.5%)
Government should take legal measures on criminals	-	4 (9.5%)
Government should control or avoid unfair or biased conflict management practices exercised by elders and clan leaders	5 (10.4%)	2 (4.8%)
Strengthen the traditional participation of communities in resolving social problems	2 (4.2%)	6 (14.3%)
Place government peace keeping force to take immediate action	-	10 (23.8%)
Enable the society to involve in off/non-farm activities	9 (18.8%)	-
Improve government policy on use of grazing land and water	9 (18.8 %)	-
Increase people's awareness on peace and security through intensive training	2 (4.2%)	-
All concerned parties need to deal with each other in finding out appropriate solutions	5 (10.4%)	-

SOURCE: Own survey, August 2010

In the opinion of one pastoralist named Hamedo, the first measure to deal with conflicts should be rejecting harmful traditions like 'an eye-for-an eye' kind of avenging. According to this informant, handling the problem through formal legal court procedures should be considered a second alternative. Of course, this tradition would take many years to change but actions should start now. For example, according to the *Axuma* culture of Afar, all Afar girls are already engaged to husbands at an early age and are not free to choose their husbands when they become grown ups. Changing this cultural practice would require a relatively long period and strong and continuous consultative dialogue among the concerned community leaders, clan elders, religious scholars, secular scholars, women, men, and the youth.

Key informants also suggested that there is a need for strengthening the capacity of the Afar Regional government and maintain good governance through holding joint conferences among regional governments and bordering *woreda* to exchange ideas and develop strategies to reduce conflicts and ultimately minimize ethnic mistrusts. The informants are also of the opinion that in the long run transformation of the pastoral system into a market-oriented sedentary economic system would be instrumental to halt ethnic conflicts and lead to integration of pastoral and highland economies.

Most discussants suggested two approaches to mitigate or eliminate tradition-based and resource-related conflicts. Some more details are provided below.

a. Economic engagement

An important strategy to mitigate conflicts is to engage the people in economic activities and employment, which influence people to think of gaining more profit and wealth by engaging in efficient and productive activities. Creating and expanding employment opportunities for Afar pastoralists in various productive sectors will help them to change their attitude from one of avenging towards thinking to become better-off in wellbeing and wealth creation. According to informants, there is an increasing trend in the decline of conflicts as Afar youth become engaged in economic activities and modern schooling. A key factor that helps economic activities and interaction is expansion of road connection and means of transportation both of which require considerable investment. Having good roads and transportation services that connect Awash-Dulecha-Aliyu Amba-Ankober with Debreberhan, on the one hand, and one that connects Kumame-Abayaatir-Shewarobit (local development corridor), on the other hand, would be very instrumental to expand economic engagement and market interaction among diverse cultural groups and contribute to reduction of incidences of conflicts.

b. Cultural change

Stopping undesired songs during circumcision ceremony: Songs during circumcision in which the heroism of the father is narrated in front of the invited guests that includes declaration of the father's achievement and patriotism by citing the number of non-Afar or Amharas he killed must be avoided.

Avoiding putting on decorative symbols: There are decorative symbols, such as material items that are put on the traditional defense weapons (e.g. *Gillie*), hand bracelets, finger rings, etc. to show that the person is a hero who has killed his or his clan's enemies. Rejecting and condemning such harmful traditional practices by the Afar communities would help to mitigate or eliminate ethnic oriented conflict.

Avoiding undesired and harmful practices during marriage process: Males who want to marry are expected to kill the 'enemies' of their family or clan and demonstrate their heroism and masculinity. Thus condemning and eliminating such requirement as socially undesired traditional practices would help to mitigate conflicts. A fundamental measure that needs to be seriously considered is the expansion of education as it is a key instrument to speed up positive economic and cultural changes.

An important measure taken in relation to conflict management by Afar regional government and the regional council has been rewriting the customary rules of conflict management and introducing penalties in such a way that they do not contradict with the modern regional and national laws and regulations. Agreements have been reached among the concerned *woredas* on the rules and penalties against those who raid animals. The agreements include transferring suspected offenders to respective *woredas* where the violations were committed. Another important measure taken by the Afar regional government is appointing peace committee members as salaried advisers to Afar regional councilors.

6.   Concluding Remarks

The concluding points presented in this section are based on the findings discussed and observations made earlier. The main objective of the study was to assess the status of economic interactions between the pastoral and highland economic systems in Northeastern Ethiopia on the basis of two cases of pastoral *woredas* in the Afar region. The *woredas* were selected purposively to ensure that they are sub-adjacent to neighboring highland *woredas*, which happened to be in North Shewa zone. The economic basis of the two case *woredas* is pastoral and to a limited extent agro-pastoral activities are also practiced. The pastoral *woredas* suffer from drought and shortage of water and pasture while the highland population ekes out a meager life from degraded mountainous farmlands, particularly in Ankober *woreda*. The Kewot *woreda* is largely lowland and increases in its elevation as one goes beyond the *woreda* town, Shwarobit, towards the west. Shewarobit is the market center for pastoralists, farmers and urban communities. Pastoralists in both *woredas* do supply livestock, particularly goat and cattle to highland towns like Shewarobit, which is supplied by SRG pastoralists and Aliyu Amba town by Dulecha pastoralists. Agro-pastoralists from Argoba Liyu *woreda* and farmers from Ankober also supply their products and purchase commodities of pastoral origin from Aliyuamba town market. These interactions have been in practice for a long time albeit in a fragmented and irregular manner due to various constraints, including poor transportation and road connections, and pasture-water resource-related and traditional culture-based conflicts among different ethnic and socio-cultural groups of the Afar, Amhara, Argoba and Oromo communities.

The other factor that constrains market interactions between communities has been low production and productivity of both pastoral and highland farming systems. Both systems are based on traditional methods of rain-fed production. Use of modern productive technologies by both systems is very limited. Because of these reasons, input supply is highly constrained. Limited efforts in the institutional development of appropriate pastoral and agricultural technologies and weak technology dissemination service to pastoral system have also proved barriers to growth of production and productivity indirectly hampering market linkage between the pastoral and highland economic systems.

The poor market infrastructure and weak institutions are also fundamental problems that hinder free exchange of and interactions of pastoralists and highland farmers, traders and consumers. In sum, poorly organized market places; shortage of transportation aggravated by rugged topography in the case of Ankober-Dulecha area; lack of a thorough market inspection and policing; lack of easy and simplified means of information channeling to pastoralists, farmers, traders and consumers are also bottlenecks to economic interactions of pastoral and highland economic systems.

The study has also diagnosed the available opportunities for better economic linkages between the pastoral and highland economic systems. The pastoralists seem to have stronger inclination to engage in livestock and livestock production to be supplied to the market. This has been partially possible because some of the traditional taboos like no sale of camel or cattle milk is gradually becoming less important. Besides, young pastoralists are becoming more business oriented. The highland farmers are also showing stronger interest for market production by growing cash crops like vegetables, such as onion, cabbages and carrot, in and around Ankober and Shewarobit areas. The highland farmers also have interest in the lowland oxen for draught and goats for meat, and in the ropes pastoralists supply to markets in the highlands. The lowland pastoralists do as well show changes in their food habits towards grain-based food and demanding for more grains from highlanders. Some efforts now underway to strengthen road connection between the lowland and highland areas and improve market infrastructure both in the highland and lowland economic systems and the activities of peace committees in the sub-adjacent *woredas* are all important conditions that contribute to strengthening of the economic linkage between the pastoral and highland economic systems.

The following paragraphs reflect on conflicts as a barrier to interaction of pastoral and highland economic systems and on interventions needed to ameliorate the situation. As pointed out earlier, the major sources of conflicts among Afar, Amhara and Argoba communities are competition over water and pasture; the culture of revenge; and social disjunctions. Lack of sufficient and accessible economic engagements directly and indirectly contribute to the emergence of conflicts.

In order to meet objectives of conflict mitigation, economic growth and market development, government institutions need to be strong, committed and effective. Otherwise, it will be difficult to implement development plans. In this regard, re-examining the appropriateness and practices of existing conflict mitigating mechanisms and institutions and improving upon them are essential steps. Formal government institutions and laws need to be in place to control and penalize all kinds of offenders as per the existing laws of the country.

On the other hand, it is a fact that the existing cultural practices in operation for centuries and endorsed by the majority of the people are too strong to be easily replaced by formal institutions and rules. Both institutions are competing forces and the modern ones will only replace the traditional cultural rules and norms gradually and only when the modern institutions have enough capacity for enforcing rules and laws with sufficient efficiency, effectiveness and power. In this context, both rules and institutions may co-exist for some time but gradually the modern modifying and ultimately eroding out the traditional norms and practices. In order to hasten the replacement of the traditional by the modern, strong capacity building and proliferation and flourishing of modern institutions that have power to implement the modern laws and rules are essential. In this institutional change, development-enhancing traditions and practices of the pastoral communities need to be consulted and incorporated in order to enrich and facilitate the change process. Simultaneously, strong and consistent efforts to change the cultural attitudes towards harmful tradition and practices need to be done along with strong promotion of education for all. In this regard, the role of road infrastructure and communication and transportation services is immense. Localities and *woredas* need not be isolated, and efforts to interconnect all *kebeles* and *woredas* with centers of market are crucial. Infrastructure development can break barriers of communication and enhance ambitions to be better-off in wellbeing and wealth and help grow fast.

Considerations for future studies: This study is one of the first attempts to investigate lowland and highland economic interactions in Ethiopia. It has raised the importance of economic interactions in mitigating inter-ethnic conflicts and in enhancing sustainable livelihoods of pastoralists. While it attempted to assess the overall situation of economic interaction between lowland and highland communities, it does not claim to be an exhaustive study of the phenomena neither does it claim to provide answers for all the issues surrounding the nexus between economic interactions and mitigation of conflicts.

Simply put, the study has not addressed all aspects of the issues raised due to lack of data and time constraint. Among other things, it has not estimated the size, types of goods and services traded between the two communities on the basis of longitudinal data. It has not as well seen the relation from the highlanders' point of view except some anecdotal views gathered from some highland farmers and experts working in these areas. The study has not identified and assessed different economic and social factors of interactions between pastoralists and highland farmers. For example, the impacts of variables, such as education, wealth, gender, social relations between highland farmers and lowland pastoralists in economic interactions have not been fully addressed. The pattern of interethnic conflicts between these specific communities over long periods and the causes associated with them need further investigation. It is strongly suggested that all the preceding issues or gaps deserve attention in future research on lowland and highland economic interactions; and their role in the mitigation of inter-ethnic conflicts and promotion of sustainable pastoral livelihoods.

References

Akmel Mohammed (2010). The Vitality of Local Institutions of Conflict
    Resolution among the Afar: The case of Samu Robi Gala'lo *woreda*. M.A.
    thesis for Institute of Ethiopian Studies, Addis Ababa University

Ayalew Gebre, 2001. Pastoralism under Pressure: Land Alienation and Pastoral
    Transformations among the Karrayu of Eastern Ethiopia, 1941 to the
    Present. The Netherlands: Shaker Publishing BV. CSA, 2008. Statistical
    Abstract of the 2007 Population and Housing Census of Ethiopia: Addis
    Ababa.

Fassil Kebebew, Diress Tsegaye & Synnevag, G. 2001. Traditional coping
    strategies of the Afar and Borana Pastoralists in response to drought. Dry
    lands co ordinations group and Noragric Report No. 17 (11, 2001).

Getachew Kassa, 2000. "Dimensions of Pastoral Poverty in Ethiopia," In: Yonas
    Admassu (ed.), Proceedings of the Second National Conference on
    Pastoral Development in Ethiopia, Poverty Reduction Strategy and
    Pastoral Development, pp. 66 -80, organized by Pastoralist Forum
    Ethiopia, Imperial Hotel, Addis Ababa, May 22 -23, 2001. Addis Ababa:
    Image Enterprise Private Limited Co.

Getachew Legese, Hailemariam Teklewold, Dawit Alemu & Asfaw Negassa,
    2008. Live animal and meat export value chains for selected areas in
    Ethiopia: Constraints and opportunities for enhancing meat exports.
    Improving Market Opportunities, Discussion Paper No. 12. International
    Livestock Research Institute.

Helland, J. 1980. *Five Essays on the Study of Pastoralists and the Development
    of Pastoralism.* African Savannah studies Occasional paper No.20.
    Bergen: Socialantropologisk Institutt, Universitet I Bergen.

Hogg, Richard, 1993.   "Government Policy and Pastoralism: Some Cultural
    Issues". Conference on Pastoralism in Ethiopia, Ministry of Agriculture,
    Addis Ababa.

IDS (Institute of Development Studies), 2006. Vulnerable Livelihoods in Somali
    region, Ethiopia. IDS Research Report 57.

Kejela Getessa, Bezabih Emana & Waktole Tiki, 2006. Livelihood
    Diversification in Borana Pastoral Communities of Ethiopia: Prospects and
    Challenges.

Little, P.D., Behnke, R., McPeak, J. & Getchew Gebru, 2010. Retrospective
    Assessment of Pastoral Policies in Ethiopia, 1991- 2008. Report Number

1, Pastoral Economic Growth and Development Policy Assessment, Ethiopia.

MoFED (Ministry of Finance and Economic Development), 2005. Ethiopia: Building on Progress, A Plan for Accelerated and Sustained Development to End Poverty (PASDEP). Volume I: Main Text. Addis Ababa.

Muluken Elias, 2009. Market Access and Livelihood Diversification in Rural areas: A case study in Kewet *woreda*, North Shoa Zone, Ethiopia. M.A. thesis for Collage of Development Studies, Addis Ababa University (unpublished).

Osterloh, S. M., McPeak, J.G., Hussein Mahmoud, Luseno, W.K., Little, P.D., Getachew Gebru & Barrett, C.B., 2003. Pastoralist Livestock Marketing Behavior in Northern Kenya and Southern Ethiopia: An Analysis of Constraints Limitting Off-Take Rates.

PFE (Pastoralist Forum Ethiopia), 2004. Pastoral Development in Ethiopia. Proceedings of the Third National Conference on Pastoral Development in Ethiopia: Pastoralism and Sustainable Pastoral Development. December 23-24, 2004, Addis Ababa

SOS Sahel Ethiopia, 2008. Pastoralism in Ethiopia: Its total economic values and development challenges.

Workneh Negatu, 2010. Lowland-Highland Relationships and Pastoral Economic Growth and Welfare. A *p*aper written as a background note for a study of "Pastoral economic growth and development in Ethiopia" that was commissioned by the Department for International Development (DfID) at the request of the Government of Ethiopia.

Workneh Negatu, Getachew Kassa, Negussie Dejene, Degefa Tolossa, Tesfaye Tafesse & Ali Hassen, 2009. Report on the Status of Pastoralism in Ethiopia. Oxfam, GB. (unpublished, monograph).

Workneh Negatu, 2006: *Pastoral Development Policies and Strategies in Ethiopia; Retrospect and Prospect. Draft Paper prepared for Conference on Pastoral Development in Ethiopia,* Addis Ababa, Institute of Development Research/Addis Ababa University (IDR/AAU).

UN OCHA- PCI (2007), Risk Taking for Living: Trade and Marketing in Somali Region of Ethiopia. Addis Ababa, Ethiopia.

Appendix

Appendix Table 1: Animals of Amhara (Sefiberet, Kureberet, Abaya-ater and Debrena-Jegol Kebeles) raided by Afar (Asgefen and Harehamo kebeles)

No.	Animal Types	2009/10		2008/09		2007/08	
		Number raided	Number returned	Number raided	Number returned	Number raided	Number returned
1	Cattle	70	42	133	72	63	-
2	Camel	13	4	14	6	39	-
3	Donkey	20	3	8	1	-	-
4	Calves			4	2	-	-
5	Shoats			50	7	50	-
6	Paid in *Birr*	2,800.00		6000.00		13, 500.00	

SOURCE: Kewot *Woreda* Office of Administration and Security Affairs, Annual reports for year 2009/10 (2002 FY, Eth. Cal), 2008/09 and 2007/08

Appendix Table 2: Animals of Afar raided by Amhara individuals

No.	Animal Types	2009/10		2008/09		2007/08	
		Number raided	Number returned	Number raided	Number returned	Number raided	Number returned
1	Cattle	6	6	25	23	18	-
2	Camel	3	2	7	7	20	-
3	Donkey	-	-	-	-	-	-
4	Calves	-	-	2	2	-	45
5	Shoats	-	-	2	2	-	5
6	Paid in *Birr*	26, 500.00		3,500.00		16, 000.00	

SOURCE; Kewot *Woreda* Office of Administration and Security Affairs, Annual reports for year 2009/10 (2002 FY, Eth. Cal), 2008/09 and 2007/08

Appendix 3: Checklist for FGD and key informants interviews for pastoral communities in SRG and Dulecha *woredas*

1. Livelihood activities

1.1   Types of on-farm and off/non-farm activities, and level of their income contributions, sufficiency for sustainable livelihood

1.2   Trends and constraints to non/off-farm livelihood activities in terms of ensuring sustainable livelihoods;

1.3   Problems encountered in off/non-farm activities;

1.4   Suggestions to solve the problems

2. Market linkages and markets situations

2.1   Products sold by pastoralists, how frequently

2.2   Products, commodities, or services produced by highlanders and purchased or obtained by lowland pastoralists from highland town and market centers or from lowland town and market

2.3   The whereabouts and infrastructure situation of the markets visited by pastoralists: market place; shades, sufficiency of space, water, telephone, electricity means of transportation, stores, laborers availability, security, availability of inspection of product quality

2.4   Any *Kebele* or *woreda/zone* or region level institutions/bodies organizations involved in the market and market infrastructure development, and in administration, security protection of marketplaces and market participants

1.4   Your views on market orientation of pastoralists/agro-pastoralists

3. Constraints to market and economic interactions between pastoralists and highland farmers

2.1   Market accessibility, production-related constraints, conflicts, culture and tradition related constraints and problems

4. Conflict issues

4.1   Causes

4.2   Role of pasture and water in conflicts

4.3   Committees/institutions involved in alleviating conflicts; success so far; problems faced

www.ingramcontent.com/pod-product-compliance
Lightning Source LLC
Chambersburg PA
CBHW021719210326
41599CB00013B/1695